IRON
BODY
NINJA

Also by Ashida Kim

The Invisible Ninja
Ninja Mind Control
Secrets of the Ninja

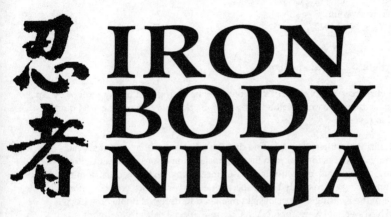

IRON BODY NINJA

The Secrets of Superior Strength

ASHIDA KIM

Citadel Press
Kensington Publishing Corp.
www.kensingtonbooks.com

CITADEL PRESS books are published by

Kensington Publishing Corp.
850 Third Avenue
New York, NY 10022

All Kensington titles, imprints, and distributed lines are available at special quantity discounts for bulk purchases for sales promotions, premiums, fund raising, educational, or institutional use. Special book excerpts or customized printings can also be created to fit specific needs. For details, write or phone the office of the Kensington special sales manager: Kensington Publishing Corp., 850 Third Avenue, New York, NY 10022, attn: Special Sales Department, phone 1-800-221-2647.

Kensington and the K logo Reg. U.S. Pat. & TM Office
Citadel Press is a trademark of Kensington Publishing Corp.

First printing 1997

10 9 8 7 6 5 4

Printed in the United States of America

Library of Congress Cataloging-in-Publication Data

Kim, Ashida.
   Iron body ninja : the secrets of superior strength / Ashida Kim.
      p. cm.
   "A Citadel Press book."
   ISBN 0–8065–1910–X
   1. Ninjitsu.   I. Title.
GV1114.73.K56   1997
796.815—dc21   97–17779
                                                          CIP

CONTENTS

IRON
BODY
NINJA

THE LEGEND
OF THE IRON NINJA

One of the most famous of the Japanese Ninja is Sarutobi Sasuke, who was renowned for his leaping and jumping ability as well as his savage and terrifying fighting techniques. He was truly a master of the Art of Invisibility. Since it was so easy for him to evade attack and thereby prevail in any encounter, either by killing his adversary or simply disappearing, he was able to perceive the needlessness of slaying either large numbers of troops on the battlefield or even a single sentry who might bar his path. And so, being almost superhumanly powerful, he became benevolent. There are many tales of the "Monkey King Ninja" leaping over the flashing blades of dozens of samurai, taunting them by slipping in and out of range of their swords until they swarmed about in frustration, often cutting each other, only to be left with the mocking laughter of their intended prey.

Nor was Sarutobi known for assassinating the enemy warlords that ravaged feudal Japan. Again, it was not because he could not have done this easily; he preferred to use espionage. The covert gathering of intelligence and the skillful application of a small amount of force were all he needed to subvert an enemy's plan. It was one such mission that inspired the most famous legend of this mythic hero.

During a time when his clan had been declared outlaws by the shogun, Sarutobi was sent to spy on and disrupt the warlord's defenses, preparatory to an attack by his tribe, which would require a certain amount of time to organize and mount.

He had done quite well keeping the enemy busy. He set small fires that destroyed food stores which would have supplied an army or fed the people in a siege, spread rumors and dissent, poisoned the wine of the generals so that they would become ill (not ill enough to be replaced, just nullified and forced to wait), and spread mysterious "plagues" among the elite bodyguards whereby an entire squad would fall into a coma for a day or two.

One night, while gathering intelligence by eavesdropping in the shogun's attic, he was spotted by a watchful guard as he was slipping into the darkness. The alarm was sounded and the household bodyguards gave chase.

Of course, the shogun was also being helped by another famous Ninja of the time, Hanzo Hattori, which was one of the reasons, beyond political considerations, why the warlord could not simply be killed. As part of his security procedures, Hanzo had secretly set a variety of traps around the castle to prevent both intrusion and escape.

When Sarutobi, having momentarily forgotten the Ninja axiom of not looking down on the enemy, sprinted to his concealed springboard (one of the secrets of his great leaping ability), he sprang to the lip of the castle wall, ran along the edge and jumped to the other side—and suddenly found his left foot securely seized by a large bear trap. The sentries surrounded him before he could extricate his leg. So, virtually pinned to the ground, deprived of his nimble and evasive techniques, he drew his sword and fought it out with a dozen or more of the sentries before cutting off his foot, seizing the severed limb, and bolting for the surrounding forest.

Pursuit continued, since by now the whole brigade was aroused. After nearly being captured several times, Sarutobi was surrounded and on the point of being taken alive. Bloodied but unbowed, his left leg tied up in a tourniquet made from the cord of his sword, he defiantly challenged his opponents to do their worst and placed upon them the Curse of the Seven Golden Vampires. He swore to return each night and hunt them down for a most horrible and hideous revenge. Then he committed *seppuku* (ritual suicide) by driving the point of his sword into his throat to pin his jaws shut—a sign that he had not betrayed any confidence of his master—and severed his brain stem, causing almost instant and painless death. The samurai bodyguards were so outraged at being denied the prize of capturing, and subsequently torturing, the infamous "ghost-soldier" that they chopped off his head and threw his body into the castle moat.

Then the curse started to come true. Stories of the battle soon spread among the court and then to the people, who found themselves at war with a demon come back from the grave to avenge himself. Horribly mangled bodies began to appear around the city. Things were very tense.

Meanwhile, back at the home clan, reports of these events kept coming in. The army was raised, and an assault, with all expectations of victory, was launched. Unfortunately, the battle did not quite go according to plan. The shogun's forces were well prepared and decimated the Sasuke clan. How could this have happened with a "demon" on their side? And against a demoralized enemy?

Some said it was because Sarutobi's curse was only for personal revenge and that the war was lost the moment he fell in battle. But later historians found that it was Hanzo, acting as Sarutobi, who gave rise to the fulfillment of the curse, and that some of those killed had only been reported to have been massacred. Of course, some actually were brutalized, since the shogun was not above killing off a few internal enemies and letting the blame fall on a ghost. But it should be noted that even after his demise, there were new stories of Sarutobi and his exploits, which suggested that later events were attributed to him, that someone else posed as him, or, for the true believer, that he had not died after all.

All of this raises the question: how could any man train himself to such a level to accomplish this in a single lifetime? The answer is found in the secret breathing techniques of the Ninja meditation system, which form the foundation for every other aspect of the art. And these are far more ancient than even the Ninja of feudal Japan were willing to accept.

There is considerable resistance among the Japanese to

acknowledge any outside influences on their lifestyle or their
martial arts. However, to those who have studied the *toramaki*
(sacred scrolls) of the Japanese system, it is quite apparent that
they are largely based on Chinese concepts of warfare dating
back to Sun Tsu, several centuries before. But even Sun Tsu's
analysis of battlefield and espionage stratagems is not the first
text on the subject. (It not only predates, but, if read carefully,
can be seen as the basis for the Western classic *On War* by Karl
Clausewitz, used by almost all military academies.)

The origins of the Ninja breathing techniques go back even
further, to a time when all knowledge, all teaching, was
transmitted by oral tradition, to the earliest civilizations of
Mesopotamia, Persia, and Egypt, to the first tribes of the Indus
Valley, and a culture known in anthropological circles as the
Jain. (They are frequently referred to by the late Joseph Camp-
bell as some of the original peoples of the Earth with an
organized society.)

Other writers have found this connection, notably Eric von
Lustbader, who authored a series of novels on Ninjitsu and
moved on to a set of more arcane martial art. He refers to this
ancestral tribe as the Jian and ascribes to them fantastic mental
and physical abilities far beyond those of mortal men. He
recognizes that the Jain were still only remnants of an even
earlier world population wiped out about forty-three thousand
years ago by planetary events like the reversal of the magnetic
poles, and that these were only followers of an even more
ancient teaching handed down by oral tradition for centuries
before them. These were the real keepers of the Secret Knowledge from that lost time.

The core of this secret knowledge had to do with their deep
and profound understanding of themselves and the pattern of
the Universe as expressed in Nature, so they were not at the
mercy of the elements, each other, or even the ravages of time.
It was in this selfsame secret knowledge that Ninjitsu had its
origins—though much has been lost and distorted with time
and transmission to the present day—in particular the secret
breathing techniques of the Ninja meditation system. Knowledge and practice of these ancient and arcane arts enabled

Sasuke Sarutobi, the Iron Ninja, to run faster than a speeding arrow, bend steel in his bare hands, and scale sheer walls like a fly. He could also endure hours of hiding in cramped places, go without food or water, withstand incredible pain, and have the force of will not to be taken alive. These exercises most likely fostered a quite real belief on the part of Sarutobi that he could and would come back and make good on his dying threat. Some say he did, albeit through the actions of Hanzo Hattori, who may have acted alone, seizing the opportunity to concoct his own plot; or who was possessed by the ghost of Sarutobi and forced to carry out his bidding. He may even have been acting in the name of the "big picture," and done what he did simply to enhance the reputation and mystery surrounding the mystic brotherhood of the Ninja, to which both he and Sarutobi belonged and in whose service his comrade had perished. After all, clan loyalty was often stronger than any minor agreement entered into with one outside the Circle. This included even a shogun, who, like all kings and princes, is at best or worse a temporary inconvenience.

Here in this book are the means and methods of achieving such a degree of mental and physical well-being that anything is possible, even immortality, depending on the patience, perseverance, and practice of the student.

Before beginning the exercises, the student should understand their historical origins and derivation. Then he may also better understand the veracity of the techniques—first because they have survived since antiquity, and secondly because they have not appreciably changed since they were first set down.

Ninjitsu, as we call it today, has its foundation in the teachings of the Pole Star School, known to Chinese historians as having been extant some six thousand years ago in Tibet. Even today, monks of that region practice the techniques set forth in this book, among others, in order to endure the cold and hardship of the mountain peaks.

As these teachings spread over China and India, a process requiring some centuries, those who found this knowledge and shared it with others were considered sages. Few ever really grasped all the teachings. But those who perceived the pattern of Nature and the Universe could accurately predict wind, rain, famine, drought, or flood. This led many to attribute to them mystical powers beyond those of mere mortals. And certainly, to primitive man, the ability to anticipate the workings of Nature, to better plant, hunt, and forage, was greatly prized and virtually essential to survival.

Of course, for those who had the time and patience, such as hermits, there was a greater goal to be achieved: self-actualization, which made things like enduring pain or having inhuman strength in a crisis mere child's play. Naturally, such powers are within the grasp of any human being. This is what the sages always told their pupils, just as magicians do today: "I have no magic power. Anyone can do what I do, if they but know how."

The true experience of such rapture is, of course, transcendental, and therefore difficult to describe in words or even pictures. The trick is that it can be *experienced* by practicing the exercises which follow. But because the goal of these physical practices is of a transcendental nature, it is often expressed in symbolic terms, which are understood on a subconscious level even if the "sermon" goes "over the head" of the parishioner.

That is where Ko Hung comes in. He was a sage, circa A.D. 300, who wrote many texts on anatomy and Chinese medicine. His explanation of this experience of transcendental meditation, written in the poetic form of his day, was the basis for a whole school of ancient Chinese triads, or tongs, and was based on the principle of being able to become invisible and kill one's enemies without fail or mercy, however mighty the enemy's resistance. It must be remembered that this was a period when warring gangs held their tribes and territories together through force of arms and sheer will. Such a "magical" or "demonic" enemy was therefore better to avoid and certainly not to be angered.

Ko Hung's method was considered alchemy, but not of the modern definition, which is associated with sorcery. Rather, it was the study of all the sciences known at that time, of which there were precious few. Hence the term "all-chem[istr]y." What he taught was the chemistry of the human body, namely, how to turn the food we eat, the water we drink, and even the air we breathe, into the best essential elements for good health and longevity. Even though he was speaking symbolically when he promised "invisibility" and "invulnerability to fang and claw," those abilities do come from doing these arcane exercises.

Upon his passing, Ko Hung was designated an immortal by the Chinese who lived on to tell of him, as is their custom with men of great knowledge who are widely known and revered, so that others will follow their example (there are Eight Immortals in the Taoist system of reckoning).

Even before he was designated an Immortal, however, Ko Hung's mortal lifespan was quite long. Some say he attained several hundred years of age. One of the reasons he lived so long was that he knew how to relax—a skill somewhat rare in a primitive world of warring kingdoms.

Ko Hung was able to relax partly because he knew that nothing he did was of any real consequence to the flow of the Universe, and partly because he knew how to "push the buttons" that activated whatever endocrine gland was necessary to stimulate an organ to produce a desired effect. He could use endorphins to withstand pain, adrenalin to lift a huge rock off a child's leg, or simply the energy necessary to let the pressures of daily survival—finding enough food without being killed—become of no account. Surely, if Ko Hung could do that, modern man should be able to relieve some of his daily stress by the same means.

Therefore, the first exercise is called Sighing. It is the first in a series of breath regulating exercises called Qi Gong (cheegung). All other breathing exercises, which are also a part of Qi Gong, are derived from it, regardless of how complicated they may appear.

Likewise, in the physical exercises, the key to all yoga, be it Indian or Chinese, is mental control of the endocrine system. Through these movements, as described by Ko Hung and in more recent times Li Ch'ing, the student progressively gains mental control of each endocrine gland in sequence, from bottom to top, until the pineal gland, deep within the brain, is reached. As Ko Hung points out, this cannot be accomplished in a day, but once it is the organs can be stimulated to increase internal body heat to withstand cold, or acquire any of the other powers already mentioned. That is why these exercises are taught in a progressive series from Stillness (Sighing) to those which develop mental control of the glands (Deer, Crane, and Turtle), to those which are used for maintaining the physical body (the Longevity Exercise).

These include the Pranayama (Hindu) or Qi Gong (Chinese) breathing exercises, which provide the student with a "grand tour" of the physical self (the Inner Journey). Together, these physical and meditative exercises lead to a state of such calm and well-being that one is said to have developed the Body of Jade—a state of virtual suspended animation completely impervious to the outside world and at once in touch with the Inner Self and the Cosmic Consciousness.

Man was not meant to remain in such a state indefinitely, although Da Mo, the "big monk," or Bodhiharma responsible for some of these exercises, was said to have meditated on a rock outside his temple for ten straight years using this method. This was so long, in fact, that there is still today such a stone in Honan Province with his shadow etched into it. But even he eventually came back to the "real" world and shared what he had discovered in the form of movements that develop tendon strength and circulate the vital energy of the body. It is these which transmute the normal human body into one which has "bones like iron," just as the other therapeutic exercises develop organs and muscles, and breathing develops the mental control and will to use them.

Many other schools of martial art teach their own version of Iron Body, but many have also gone far afield from its original purpose. In Japanese Karate schools such as the Shotokan, for example, students are often taught to deaden the nerves in their forearms so that they can withstand the impact of blocking powerful strikes from an opponent. This is a type of Iron Body, but one detrimental to the muscles and bones leading to the hand.

In Thai kickboxing, fighters sometimes have the nerves which register pain in the legs severed surgically so they can deliver powerful kicks without fear of pain. One way to practice this is to kick with full force against a live tree until the tree dies or the leg is broken—again, detrimental to good health in one's old age.

Similarly, in Korean Hapkido, an advanced level of Tae Kwon Do, students receive training in how to defend themselves with a cane. This is because if they live long enough, most will need a cane to walk on feet crippled by years of impact practice.

In some Chinese martial arts there are specific techniques used to develop the Iron Vest, which enables the user to protect his internal organs from both pressure point (Dim Mak or Death Touch) strikes and to withstand the relatively blunt trauma of other blows. The training method involves beating the body with progressively more solid objects and eventually flailing oneself with an "iron broom." This latter device is constructed by binding a series of short metal rods, much like straightened out coat hangers, to a stick so that it looks like a broom. (This is much like the method of developing the "iron palm," which involves striking padded targets, then punching devices wrapped with rope, and then the bare wood or metal beneath the training aids.)

The idea is that by striking himself with ever increasing force so that he has control of how much impact is felt, the student will learn to instinctively tighten up at the moment of impact, and so will be able to escape injury—at least until the cumulative effects of all this self-flagellation catch up with him in old age. The classic test for Iron Vest Kung Fu is to jump off an eight-foot wall and land on the chest without injury, thus demonstrating the amount of impact that can be absorbed. This, more than most other tests, shows one is closer to the true Iron Body, but it is still off the mark.

True practitioners of Qi Gong learn such complete control of their anatomy that they do not tense up at the moment of impact, only for a second at the *site* of impact, and even then only long enough to repel the blow. If they tightened their whole body it would slow them down from counterpunching.

This reinforces the principle of being relaxed so that one can move quicker and more spontaneously than if he is already braced for impact. In that case, the tensed muscles must relax before they can respond to a mental command to strike out. That is one of the reasons we keep talking about relaxation as an integral part, not only of meditation, but of Iron Body.

Some Kung Fu schools speak at great length of "directing the Qi" to the site of the impact, and offer exercises like using a loose fist to strike the body at various points and in various patterns to develop this technique. But even that is unnecessary when the body is healthy and the channels of circulation are functioning properly. When that is the case, the body responds spontaneously and automatically to any blow. Consider for a moment: When one receives a small cut on the finger, does the entire body bleed? Do all the blood vessels constrict? Are clotting agents sent to every part of the body? No, only those needed to deal with the site of the injury—the same with Qi and the Iron Body.

You see, the human body is capable of far more than most doctors are even aware of. So most of these high-impact Iron Body methods are completely unnecessary, as indicated in the discussion of how things get lost and modified through time and different instructorship. The student of Ninjitsu Iron Body, then, must begin at the beginning. This means learning a few "signposts" and "landmarks," such as the Five Element Theory and the Map of the Body. This will include the Eight Psychic Channels and the twelve meridians of acupuncture.

But don't worry. It isn't as complicated as it sounds or as many "scholars" would have us believe. Besides, the ancients, in their infinite wisdom, have provided us with simple mnemonic devices with which to remember all this, namely, the fingers. And, part of the breathing exercises and the Grand Psychic Tour of the body is to imagine each of these bilateral channels in a logical sequence as you breathe in and out, making them easy to remember. It will be seen that just as all breathing exercises come from sighing and all longevity exercises come from the deer, crane, and turtle, these channels start with one small circulation, move to a simple bilateral circulation, then expand to an eight-branched circulation, and on to the twelve meridians. By the time you get there it will be, as stated before, child's play.

Throughout the book, Chinese, rather than Japanese, terminology has been employed for clarity.

Finally, remember the axiom, "Never look down on your opponent [feel superior to him] and never look up at him [feel inferior] lest you be overcome with confidence or insecurity. Everyone has an equal chance in the Game of Life and Death."

Doing these exercises will not make you "better" than anyone else. But they will make you better than you are now in terms of health, longevity, and understanding. And it is difficult to find a more noble mission than that.

BREATHING, MEDITATION, AND IMMORTALITY

I cannot describe to you the indescribable, but I can teach you several by no means inconsiderable arts—invisibility, flying without wings, invulnerability to sword or serpent's fang—you know the kind of thing.

Here then is your syllabus of study. Seeking the mysterious portal, you must first provide yourself with the wherewithal to bribe the guards and render yourself invisible so that you may slip through unnoticed. That sort of thing is not mastered in a day.

Next, you will have to learn to fly henceforth to the courts of Heaven, make your way to the central chamber, surprise Lord Lao at breakfast, snatch up his flask of Golden Elixir, slay those who will come running to rescue it, break down the wall of the sky-castle and return to Earth an Immortal!

A man of your determination has but to follow my course of instruction to be certain of success.

—from the Nei Pien of Ko Hung, an ancient treatise on alchemy, medicine, and religion, A.D. 320.

THE WISDOM OF KO HUNG

The ancient masters knew that to be truly spiritual and lead an exemplary life one must be above and beyond the gross temptations, such as money, of ordinary men. Therefore, the "price" they extracted from their students, who were carefully screened for proper moral and ethical standards before being given the gift of enlightenment, was a promise: If they achieved some modicum of success through these exercises, which would turn them into sages, they would neither become so disenchanted with the sorry state of worldly affairs nor so eager to experience continual bliss that they would kill themselves or allow themselves to die before passing on their knowledge to at least ten others. This not only fulfilled the unconscious wish of the applicant, i.e., that there was no monetary cost and that his previous devotion had not been in vain. It also gave him a purpose, even in his darkest hour, and a reason to keep practicing.

"Flying without wings" represents the physiological sensation elicited by the Deer, Crane, and Turtle exercises, which will be introduced on p. 37. When these exercises are performed properly, there is a distinct sensation, beginning at the base of the spine, which runs up the back and floods over the top of the head. The student feels like he is flying, which symbolically he is, to the Sky Palace or Mind Fortress—in psychological terms, the "secret place," usually a childhood memory, where one retreats in times of stress. On the physical plane this is represented as the skull and brain.

The secret of invisibility is Stillness. That is why the practice begins by sitting quietly so that later, when performing the Inner Journey, one can focus on the internal sounds of the body and be oblivious to the outside world. This requires concentration and patience, two of the skills taught in the practice that "go with the territory," whether the student sought to learn them or not.

Like so many things expressed metaphysically, one can then "slip through the Mysterious Portal." Of course, the transcendental nature of the experience is that the student does not actually move to enter this "gate." Instead, reaching the Precious Square Inch (also known as the Third Eye in Yoga) means one has stimulated the uppermost endocrine gland, the pineal, with the hormone-saturated blood created by the combination of the breathing exercises (which alter the pH of the blood) and the mental control gained from the "internal pump" exercises (these are also called chakras, or energy wheels, in Yoga). That blood is circulated under conscious direction. The exercises include the sacral pump, performed by squeezing the buttocks together, or, as is more commonly taught, tensing the muscles of the Tan T'ien, or lower belly. Tensing the Tan T'ien has the corollary effect of tightening the buttocks, but is a phraseology one can use in more polite company—one of the big secrets or Qi Gong and Yoga.

The next exercise focuses on the heart, which operates without conscious direction but which can be sped up or slowed down merely by regulating the rate of respiration. And then comes the Cranial Pump Exercise, performed by pressing the tip of the tongue to the roof of the mouth. The Cranial Pump exerts a subtle pressure against the underside of the brain pan and therefore against the pineal gland, which is what we are striving to stimulate.

"Snatching the Golden Elixir From Lord Lao," means not stopping when you reach this threshold. (The name is a reference to Lao Tsu, author of the Tao Te Ching, circa 500 B.C., thereby predating Ko Hung by some eight hundred years. It is used here as a symbol of the psychological "internalized authority or father figure.") What will happen is that you will glimpse the Divine Light—the same thing that occurs at the moment of death, from a physiological standpoint. So if you are morally and ethically not ready, you will be afraid. But this is only your Ego, which strives for identification. To be one with the infinite, you must surrender the Ego, as taught in some disciplines, or leap boldly forward in spite of your fear, despite the danger of getting caught and the physiological thrill that results from such an act, just as a thief would, which is identical to what you will feel at this point in the exercise. By this we mean you shouldn't jump up from a deep meditation, or have a startled, jerking reaction that will disrupt the exercise of stillness. Often students meditating in Zen classes "jump" at the moment they feel as if they were "falling off the planet." The Zen master usually strikes them on the back with a bamboo sword known as a *shinai*, not hard enough to hurt them, but to discourage this reaction during future practice.

"Then you must slay the guardians who come to rescue the Elixir." These are, symbolically represented, the manifestations of your Ego, which you use to justify and rationalize your behavior in the world. These, too, must be cast off. if you are a bully, it is because you are afraid. If you are a miser, it is because you are alone. If you are a healer, it is because you are well yourself. But all must be set aside, the Ego must be left behind, to experience the transcendental. That is why the Ninja wear masks—not to hide their identity, but to diminish their Ego.

"Breaking down the walls of the Sky Palace": means recognizing that when you "wake up" and "return to the world," everything you thought was important when you began this quest will have paled into insignificance before the experience of inner peace. You will never look at the world the same way again. You will have given up your attachment to material things and, by so doing, become immune to the wiles and trickery of those who still think such things are important. However, you will understand why they act as they do, because you will remember that you were once like them. You lose nothing on this journey, you remember it all, and see it clearly for the first time. And remember, you made a vow to help at least ten of them figure it out like you did.

Thus, the secret of the Iron Body is not given to just anyone. The unscrupulous and unworthy do not have the patience to become Immortal. And those who do turn their bones to iron and their skin to jade learn as an inherent part of the exercise the ethical and moral lessons which ensure that the techniques are not misused.

This, the legend of Ko Hung and the references to the powers, or "invisibility and flying without wings" are the "kernels of truth" that underlie many of the myths and legends of Ninjitsu. Not only does it authenticate the practice, study, and transmission of Kuji Kiri long taught by our system, but also validates the historical lineage so important to most martial arts.

It is the tradition of Taoist masters not to reveal their personal history. This is not because they are, or were, secretive; it is merely because they have learned to live in the "now" and so neither dwell on the past nor anticipate the future. Thus, such documentation of who founded a style, or who taught it to whom and when, are less important than whether it is effective; and this is even less important than whether the style teaches the secrets of immortality—the true purpose of any religion—or is merely a long set of boring drills designed to subjugate the student to the will of the master.

It is much the same with the Ninja of today. They do not revel in telling war stories or bragging about their prowess in combat, because they know that on any given day, even a champion can be beat. Nor do they boast of their heritage. In the old days, when an "agent" went on a "mission" it was as if he had never been born, never grew up in his village, never married or had children or tended the fields or fished in the pond. He never existed. When he returned, it was as if he had never been gone.

Nor were these assignments frequent, arbitrary, or mandate a large body of men. One good man, in the right place, at the right time, can change the course of history. And one who has realized himself is capable of anything. It wasn't that the Ninja practiced creeping up on sentries or climbing walls. They were just in such harmony with Nature that these tasks were easy for them when the situation required. And, even with all this power, they interfered very little in the affairs of ordinary men, believing instead that in time the less enlightened would, as they had, find teachers to set them on the right path and show them their "tiger face"—their own true divine Inner Self.

Neither did they practice assassination techniques. They learned what they knew of anatomy through the study of medicine, but they knew that, "if you cut off the head of a snake, the body dies," and that "a pebble tossed in a pond makes many ripples on the surface." So they would, if they had to, "put the warlord to sleep," give him the peace he never found in the world of illusion, and thus stop an army, a war, or a tyrant. It was for this that they gained the reputation as the "invisible assassins," who could walk through walls, pass anywhere unseen, and vanish without leaving a trace, and even then it was seldom done except in self-defense of the tribe or clan.

They have always been among us. And all they want is to be left alone to practice a few simple breathing exercises so they can lead long and happy lives, because the real Ninja know that "living well is the best revenge." And, they welcome anyone who is willing to try.

NINJA ALCHEMY

Alchemy then, as thus far described by Lao Tsu and Ko Hung, is the science of transmutation; the manipulation of the nutrients absorbed by the body from food, water, and air, by means of breathing exercises and therapeutic movements, so that "the bones become iron, and the skin becomes jade." Interpreted from the ancient texts, this means that the bones are healthy, strong, and flexible—not that they actually become metal. But human bones can withstand incredible pressure, and if maintained by good nutrition and exercise, they can remain relatively free of catabolism, an effect of aging that makes them brittle.

Nor does the skin become jade. This is another example of the symbolic or poetic presentation of these mysteries. What is inferred is that the skin will be healthy and supple; any doctor worth his salt will tell you the best guard against infection is clean, unbroken skin. (Remember that, in olden days, when this term was coined, tetanus, obtained from open wounds and leading to lockjaw, was a real killer.) So this is a health-giving, life-prolonging exercise, accomplished by changing the pH of the blood by breathing so that the endocrine glands remain active and produce the hormones enabling the body to remain young and strong.

Some believe alchemy means turning lead into gold. This is a misconception created by European alchemists in feudal times, who thought translations of Chinese scrolls describing the "process of internal distillation," or transmutation, referred to the actual metals of lead, mercury, and gold, rather than the poetic symbols of internal chemistry.

It is possible, however, to atomically turn lead into gold, but that formula is not given here. What we are dealing with is using the body to "collect, cultivate, and circulate the Qi—a process, anatomically, very similar to the distillation of a liqueur from an alcoholic liquor, which in turn has been distilled from any number of fruit juices. By breathing we "collect"; by altering the rate of respiration and the blood pH we refine, or "cultivate"; and the resultant chemical reaction causes the "essence" to be "boiled off," and become more potent. This "elixir" then acts as an internal medication and tonic enabling the body to accomplish more of its potential.

Therefore, Ninja alchemy—real alchemy, now that you understand the meaning of the symbols—is not a key to instant riches, because for us, it is not the metal lead that will be changed into gold, but rather the base elements of the Self and the body that will be transmuted to a higher level (becoming golden), and insure longevity.

Literature is full of tales in which the famous would gladly renounce their wealth if they could but live a little longer. They have spent themselves accumulating power and paid the price for so doing. Driven to succeed, they have run themselves into exhaustion, and now only want back the time they have wasted.

Legend also tells us of beings with extremely long life spans, most of whom lament that they have seen generations of mere mortals pass away and who feel the terrible loneliness of eternal isolation, which would probably be the case, mankind being philosophical creatures.

There was once a student in pursuit of Immortality. When asked what he would do with his time once he had achieved his goal, he replied, "work to accumulate more time increments," to which his teacher responded, "Immortality is an absolute. If it were possible to attain it, you would have been here always already. The best you can pray for is a life of two hundred to three hundred years, by which time you will be sufficiently bored to gladly pass on to the next level. And if you get that far, at least have enough humanity to share what you may discover with others." So, too, this charge is given to all who would seek to become alchemists.

Followers of the Silent Way, as this Ninja science of transmutation is known, are able to perceive the "pattern of the Universe" as described in the explanation of Ko Hung's promise. Recognize that the breath control methods and exercises that help achieve longevity and Immortality, and that provide mystic abilities such as Iron Body, are in fact natural and innate abilities.

What makes the Ninja special is that they are sentient, aware of their consciousness—their Selves—and are therefore able to apply a modicum of control and direction to this phase of their existence rather than just being at the mercy of the elements, unaware that they are possessed of this innate ability. It is this awareness of Self that makes others consider them "enlightened."

Before you were an air breather, you were a water breather, tucked safely away in the womb, all your needs fulfilled, simple though they may have been, and all your ambitions realized. Then came the trauma of birth. Suddenly you were thrust into a vacuum filled with intense light and sound. You could not breathe, your lungs emptied, and you drew in your first breath of this new world. And then it was over. A new existence had begun.

You were equipped with everything needed to survive and flourish in this new world, so you began to explore with your new senses and they have brought you to this.

Why should you have any doubt at all that it will not be the same when you die? A moment of discomfort and a new reality to explore? So, then, why not forget about being Immortal and just commit suicide, if what is to follow is so wonderful?

Because there are other people here who don't know this yet, and they need to be comforted and reassured that all will be well. They need to be taught that they are the masters of their fate and the captains of their souls. Dickens begins one of his classics by saying, "I realized that if there were to be a hero in my life, it must necessarily be me."

We have said that one cannot change the world, and this is true. But one can prolong the moment. The ancient sages of China, having long ago mastered the techniques of health and longevity, would travel the countryside in search of a kingdom or realm in which the people were happy and the prince benevolent. Presenting themselves at court, they would offer to instruct the ruler in the mysteries of immortality so that his reign might endure and his people prosper for a long time.

So, too, with any true Immortal.

We have said that one may teach whomever is chosen. But this is not a test, or any attempt to impose standards on those who would follow these teachings. Essentially, the student chooses himself. Once you begin this quest and experience the wonder of it, you will want to share it with everyone. The Japanese call this *shakabuku*, the recruiting of new members, but your enthusiasm will drive most of them away. So you will become more selective with whom you share the secret of health and long life, or the fact that you have any knowledge whatsoever about it, lest ordinary mortals think you odd or even insane. These do not want to know. Not yet.

This suggests, as has long been believed, that Immortals have some power over others. They do. It is the power of a calm mind.

Again, do not be discouraged if everyone does not immediately embrace the wisdom you will learn. These are merely the means whereby one can "look on the other side," to see what is "beyond the veil." And once this is accomplished all else begins to fall into place.

You will start to see a pattern to the Universe, and what was once a great mystery—why people act the way they do—will give way to an understanding of Self and others. Most people make life difficult for themselves and cannot accept that the secret to happiness is so simple.

With a calm mind comes acceptance, and with age comes experience. That is why one is able to cope with life's minor hardships better than another—in large part because they have seen them before, and having experienced them once, either the solution has been found or it has failed, thus prompting a repeat performance or a new solution. This is called learning by experience, and offers not only a key as to how to be of service, but also an outlet for activity, which prevents boredom.

A wise man learns from experience; an Immortal also learns from the experiences of others. In this regard, Immortals reckon the passage of time somewhat differently from mortals. They have learned that if you make yourself miserable with worry, doubt, guilt, or fear, time will drag on forever. But if you let yourself be happy, it will fly by. Therefore they live "in the moment," experiencing each second as a new adventure, rejoicing in every sunrise and marveling at the beauty of each sunset. This is because they know that every day, with slight variations, is the same, that every year has a spring, summer, fall, and winter; and that these will continue regardless of whether a person is around to see them or not. Life goes on, and as long as we are remembered we never truly die.

We could explain why this is a function of the genetic code and memory, but you will learn all that for yourself—once you start to breathe. And we could go into great detail about the formulae for regulating the breath to achieve this altered state, but it is sufficient to say that the only change in the Fourfold Breath is to inhale for nine heartbeats, hold for six, exhale for nine beats, and hold for six. (One of the breathing exercises to be given later, the Fourfold Breath consists of inhaling for four heartbeats, holding the inhalation for two heartbeats, exhaling for four heartbeats, and holding the exhalation for two more.)

Qi Gong schools are full of such mathematical equations to regulate the breath, some of them unnecessarily complicated, and each is designed to elicit a particular physiological effect, such as Iron Body, the focus of this inquiry.

Again, this could be explained in terms of adjusting the pH of the blood; the fact that in numerology 9 is the only number which "retains its identity" when multiplied, (i.e., $2 \times 9 = 18$; $1 + 8 = 9$, and so on); or that the simple mental exercise of setting the mind to focus on this task of mentally reciting the multiplication tables, for even a few minutes a day to the exclusion of all else, elicits a physiological relaxation response, only recently discovered by modern science, which provides a psychological sanctuary from the stress of modern life. But only by doing it will one truly understand. Later, there will be more on the significance of the number 9 in Shugendo, the mountain warrior doctrine of a particular Buddhist sect associated with some Ninja clans.

As even all the mystics through all the ages have proclaimed, "It cannot be explained, it can only be experienced."

WHO WANTS TO LIVE FOREVER?

An appropriate question, don't you think, for one about to embark on the quest for Immortality?

Philosophers and storytellers have considered this question for quite some time, pointing out the sheer boredom of such an experience, the heartache of seeing friends and loved ones age or die, the intense loneliness of never being able to share the secret of being Immortal with anyone. They ponder these things because they, themselves, are not Immortal. If they were, they would know that learning goes on forever, and that death is merely a part of life, and that they can share the secret with anyone they choose. After all, it is not so difficult. And finally, after however many ages or lifetimes they experience, they learn what all mortals know and do instinctively—that it is solely at their command to decide when they will pass on to the next level.

As described in the interpretation of Ko Hung, this leap to the level of enlightenment is an experience much akin to being born or dying: "You see a bright light... and feel drawn to it..." just as those who have had a near death experience report. You "slip through the Mysterious Portal" and activate the pineal gland with hormone-saturated, oxygen-rich blood. The difference is that you are not dying. The only thing that happens is that your Ego is merging with the Infinite, the Cosmic Consciousness, the Universal Mind (whatever term of whatever religion you may follow) and you have become a "child of the Universe," enlightened and understanding all. "You may see the faces or hear the voices of loved ones who have gone before, beckoning to a place where you are always safe and welcome." From there the descriptions begin to vary; some return to a childhood home, others to the arms of God.

Whether this is, as scientists claim, merely a physiological reaction resulting from oxygen deprivation to the brain, with the consequent "dumping" of the memory banks into the conscious level, or the moment when life and death hang in the balance, all such descriptions of near death experiences report a feeling of "floating up out of the physical body, to hang suspended as an astral Self." That is the moment when the will comes into play.

All who have had this experience and come back to report on it say that if there were sufficient cause, they could re-enter their bodies and return to life, sometimes sitting up on the hospital bed to proclaim to a doctor, "You don't get rid of me that easily!" A strong emotional tie, such as the desire to see one's newborn child grow up, or a similar family obligation, is often strong enough to accomplish this.

So the conclusion is, and some religions include it in their dogma, that one never passes on unless one chooses to. Some claim that you do not die "until it is your time." But, once again, the selection of that time is wholly at the discretion of the individual. This is the secret of life and death. It is not a matter of secret potions or magical elixirs. All you have to do is breathe. Through control of the breath, achieved through the practice I will describe to you, one can achieve Inner Strength, Invisibility, and Iron Body, all powers attributed to the legendary Ninja.

Of course, this method of breathing is somewhat modified from normal respiration, but even a beginner can pick it up with only a little effort. So don't be discouraged if you thought it was going to be hard. Expectations, and the lack of reality to conform to them, are a major cause of frustration. But, there is no need for frustration!

Another major stumbling block in this study is delusion. This means perceiving the reality of this moment as the reality of all moments. Change is inevitable, and even if it weren't, there is nothing you can do about it. There have always been princes and peasants, and there always will be. There has always been daylight and darkness, rain and drought, feast and famine, war and peace— and there always will be. The players may change, the length of the meteorological phenomena vary, but they are the only constant for this reality. That there is an ebb and flow to the tides of the Universe was a principle of Hermes Trismegistus, a sage of ancient Egypt who reportedly lived for over three hundred years.

Most people breathe between twelve and sixteen times per minute. Being aware of this fact will make it impossible for the student to now accurately measure his own rate of respiration. Therefore, to confirm this fact, we suggest you quietly observe others. You will find that they complete one full cycle of inhalation and exhalation between three and four times in a fifteen-second period. Multiplying this by four, the number of fifteen-second intervals in one minute, will produce the figures given above. This is the method used by nurses to record the rate of respiration, pulse, and blood pressure.

There are many reasons why people breathe too quickly, even though this rate is considered normal. But none of them are relevant. What is important is for people to learn to breathe more slowly. This is the key to longevity, good health, and enlightenment.

Close your eyes. Think of the most pleasant experience you have ever had. Your breathing slows down. Your face relaxes into a slight smile. Take a deep breath and let it out through your mouth. Relax.

These are two great secrets. The first is called meditation, which leads to relaxation. The second is called Sighing. It is a stress relieving exercise.

Listen. What do you hear? The sound of your own heartbeat? The blood rushing in your veins? The sound of your own breathing?

Breathe so slowly and deeply that you can no longer hear yourself. When you have done this, you will have taken the first step on the Moonlit Path of the Silent Way. You will have learned to relax.

You are now completely relaxed.

It feels good to be relaxed; it feels better than before.

And now each time you practice this exercise it will
    become easier and work better for you.

And now, I want you to go even deeper, to be even more
    relaxed, feeling even better.

First, you must tie up the racing horse or your thoughts...

And lock up the monkey of your mind...

So that you may hear the inner drum and the silent flute.

To accomplish this, the ancients have taught us to regulate
    the breath.

Take a deep breath.

Breathe out, and imagine the number 3, three times.

Breathe in.

Breathe out, and imagine the number 2, three times.

Breathe in.

Breathe out, and imagine the number 1, three times.

Swallow, and place the tip of your tongue against the roof
    of your mouth.

You are now at a deeper, healthier, level of mind.

A level of mind you may use for any purpose you desire.

Every day, in every way, you are becoming better and
    better...

So that you may set a good example for all.

Concentrate on the goal of meditation.

Listen not with the ear, but with the mind.

Not with the mind, but with the breath.

Let hearing stop with the ear.

Let the mind cease with its images.

Breathing means to empty oneself and wait for the will.

Will abides in the emptiness of the fasting mind.

Look into the Void. What do you see? Only darkness, utter
    and complete?

Breathe deep, the surrounding night.

Fill yourself with the emptiness.

Become one with the Void.

Here you are, bone dry and bottle empty.

Brood upon the darkness and there is no one else.

Not another voice, not a whisper.

Not the touch of a hand, nor the warmth of another heart.

Only darkness and solitude.

Eternal confinement, where all is black and silent and
    nothing stirs.

Imprisonment without judgment.

Punishment without sin.

Unless some escape can be devised.

No hope of rescue from elsewhere.

No sorrow or sympathy or pity in another soul, in another
    mind.

No doors to be opened, no locks to be turned, no bars to
    be sawn apart...

Only the deep, sable night...

In which to fumble and find nothing.

You are now at an inner level of mind...

A level of mind you may use to set up your dreaming...

And make your dreams come true.

To accomplish this, the ancients have taught us to look at
    our hands.

This unites the memory and the imagination, and makes
    us present in the Dream-Time.

Your hands are familiar objects.

You have often watched them at work and at play.

It is easy to call up their image and see them before you.

A pair of hands is all you are now...

With which to gather the scattered energies of the
    Universe...

And make your dream reality.

Circle a hand to the left and there is naught.

This is Yin, the void, the feminine, dark, mysterious force
    of emptiness.

Sweep an arm to the right and discover movement in the
    nothingness.

This is Yang, the masculine, linear, positive force of the
    will.

Circle both hands up and out to the sides as you breathe in
    deeply, and let the palms meet above your head. Breathe

out as you bring the hands, palms together, down to
   solar plexus level.
This represents Tao, the unification of mind and body,
   memory and imagination, the balance between Yin and
   Yang.
These are the means of finding your Center...
Of becoming one with the Universe...
Of harnessing the powers of your mind.
You are now completely relaxed, feeling better than before.
Every day, in every way, you are becoming better and
   better.
So that you may set a good example for all.
You have learned to focus your energy, the force of your
   will.
Now we will begin to collect, cultivate, and circulate that
   force and the energies of the Universe to create the body
   of light.
With palms together, the fingers represent the Five
   Elements—Earth, Water, Fire, Air, and Wood—whereby
   all manner of things may be accomplished.

THE FIVE ELEMENTS

Now, equipped with a historical perspective of the symbolism used in the Iron Body breathing exercises, which lead to longevity and understanding, you are ready to begin the great work of developing these magical powers through conscientious practice.

Earlier on we said that the Old Ones had provided landmarks and signposts to guide you on the Inner Journey, and promised that these would be simple and easily recalled mnemonically. The means whereby this is accomplished is by using the hands and fingers. The Chinese, from whom this system is descended, classify everything according to the Five Elements: Earth, Water, Fire, Air, and Wood.

Although disputed by empirical scientists as an example of reasoning by analogy rather than what they consider to be logical thought, it is a method that is applicable on all levels—prenatal, postnatal, and spiritual. Modern science is limited to the physical level—and has a hard time explaining even that! This suggests a certain prejudice on the part of modern science, which refuses to even consider that there may be some validity to arcane arts such as acupuncture or breath control.

So, instead of making primitive students learn the Periodic Table with some 136 or so atomic elements, as Western science has, the ancients looked at their hands and associated each of the five elements with a particular finger: Earth-pinky; Water-ring; Fire-middle; Air-index; and Wood-thumb. The left hand was considered Yin, or feminine energy, the right was designated as Yang, or masculine energy, and the ritual movements that begin this meditation practice illustrate and reinforce the memory of this primordial attempt to explain the Universe.

THE MAP OF THE HANDS

Here, then, is their Map of the Hands, which can be used for mathematical calculation, connection of the psychic channels, palmistry, astrology, and so on.

Likewise, the Map of the Body is presented so the student will be aware of the organs and bodily structures related to the symbolic instructions and recognize them when encountered on the Inner Journey.

The Five Elements, Earth, Water, Fire, Air, and Wood, encompass all the phenomena of Nature. It is a symbolism that applies itself equally to man.

MAP OF THE HANDS AND PULSES

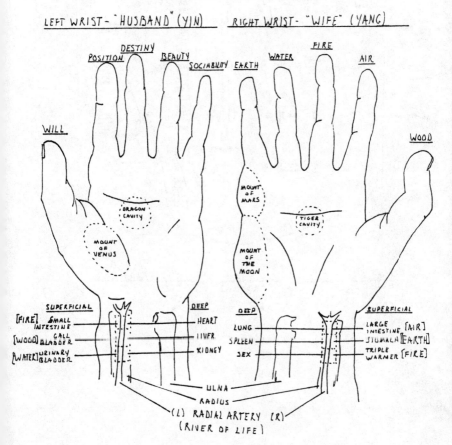

MAP OF THE BODY

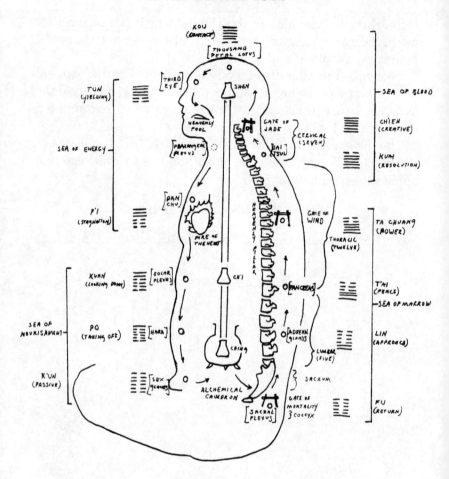

ENDOCRINE GLANDS	LOCATION	KUJI-KIRI
GONADS	SCROTUM	CHU
ADRENALS	KIDNEYS	SHEN
PANCREAS	STOMACH	TAI
THYMUS	HEART	SHA
THYROID	THROAT	JEN
PITUITARY	SPINE	TUNG
PINEAL	BRAIN	HUA

Just as things may be classified according to their Yin and Yang aspects, they may be further divided into their elemental components. These interact in specific and prescribed manners, the alteration of which is not possible and the study of which may consume a lifetime.

"Fire creates Earth (ash), which creates Air (smoke), which creates Water (condensation), which creates Wood (life), which creates Fire (energy). This is the cycle of creation. Wood destroys Earth (by covering), Fire destroys Air (by combustion), Earth destroys Water (by retention), Air destroys Wood (by smothering), Water destroys Fire (by extinguishing). This is the cycle of destruction. The Yin and Yang of Nature, the Inevitable Law of Change.

THE LAW OF THE FIVE ELEMENTS

If there is excess energy in an organ, it may be dissipated at the point of sedation for that organ. The organ which follows in the circulation of energy will then receive the excess energy and the preceding one will be sedated. Therefore the sedation point for one organ is the point of tonification for the next one in sequence.

Each organ meridian is also possessed of a master point known as the source; a "lo" point, which acts on coupled organs; a connecting point with other meridians; an approval point on the bladder meridian; an alarm point on the abdomen; an ancient control point; and a point which is "forbidden."

That which comes from behind is empty, having spent its energy in following the creative cycle; that which comes from the front is fullness, flowing against the creative; that which comes from not winning is thief and is part of the destructive cycle; that which comes from winning is minute, acting counter to the destructive flow; illness of the organ itself is called upright.

—from The Nei Ching

LAW OF THE FIVE ELEMENTS

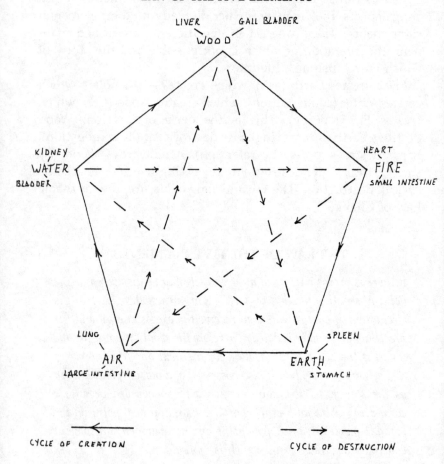

THE NEI CHING ON QI

What follows are excerpts from the world's oldest known book on medicine, which begins with the Su Wen, a transcript of conversations between Huang Ti, the Yellow Emperor of China, circa 3000 B.C., and Ch'i Po, his master physician.

HUANG TI: I have heard that in ancient times, the people lived to be over one hundred years old, and yet

IMBALANCE OF QI RESULTING IN ILLNESS

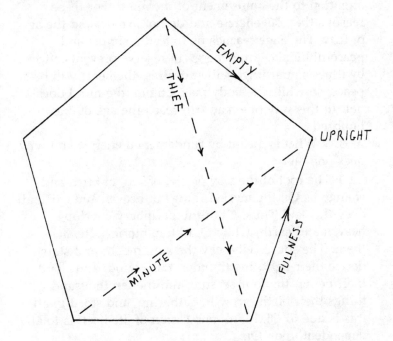

remained active and did not become decrepit in their
activities. But in our time, they only reach half that age
and become weak and failing. Is it that mankind is
degenerating through the ages and is losing its original
vigor and vitality?

CHI PO: In ancient times, the people understood the Tao,
the Great Principle of the Universe. They patterned
themselves upon the Laws of Yin and Yang, were sober
and led regular simple lives in harmony with Nature.
For these reasons, they were healthy in mind and body,
and could live to a ripe old age. In our time, they drink
alcohol as if it were water, seek all manner of physical
pleasure and abandon themselves to intemperance.
Their passions exhaust their vital forces; their cravings
dissipate their true essence; they do not know how to
find contentment within themselves; they are not skilled

in the control of their spirits and devote all their
attention to the amusement of the mind. For these
reasons they degenerate and do not live beyond the age
of fifty. The Sage teaches us to lead a simple and
peaceful life; keeping energy in reserve prevents attack
by illness; guarding against desires, the heart will be at
peace; so while the body may fatigue, the mind does
not. In this way one may still reach the age of one
hundred.

HUANG TI: What is meant by fundamental energy, and why
does one die?

CH'I PO: The root of the way of life, of Tao, of birth and
change, is Qi; the myriad things in heaven and earth all
obey this law. Thus, Qi in the periphery envelops
heaven and earth, while Qi in the interior activates
them. The source whereby the sun, moon, and stars
derive their light, the thunder, rain, wind, and cloud,
their being, the four seasons and the ten thousand
things their birth, growth, gathering, and storing, all
this is due to Qi. Man's possession of life itself is totally
dependent upon Qi.

In Heaven there is wind, in Earth there is wood; in
Heaven there is heat, in Earth there is fire; in Heaven
there is damp, in Earth there is earthiness; in Heaven
there is dryness, in Earth there is metal; in Heaven there
is cold, on Earth there is water; in Heaven there is Qi, in
Earth there is form; form and Qi interact to create the
ten thousand things.

The intercourse of Qi between Heaven and Earth
resulted in the creation of man. That which was in the
beginning in Heaven, on Earth becomes visible as form.
In the creation of man, the Life Essence (Yin) appears
first. The origin of life is in the Essence (Yang) and
when these unite it is called Spirit.

The energy coming at birth from the mother is the
fundamental energy, that from the father is secondary.
When the two energies cease, there is death. Whoever
has the Spirit flourishes, whosoever loses it perishes.

Although the Spirit is produced from Life Essence and Qi, that which governs and selects the Essence and the Qi and controls their function is the Spirit of the heart. The heart houses the Spirit; the lungs the Animal Soul; the liver the Spiritual Soul; the spleen the Mind; and the kidneys the Will.

True Qi is the original Qi from Heaven, received through the nose and controlled by the windpipe. Qi from food and water enters the stomach and is controlled by the gullet. That which nourishes the unborn is the Qi of former Heaven (prenatal, Yin); that which fills the newborn is called the Qi of latter Heaven (postnatal, Yang).

Qi is collected in the Heavenly Pool through proper breathing and meditation, allowing the energy to collect and escape. Beneath the palate, the Qi descends through the windpipe and is absorbed by the heart through the lungs. It passes down the aorta behind the solar plexus to the liver and the Hara to the Gate of Mortality at the root of the genitals. There it is joined by the Tu Mo, or Channel of Control, and ascends through the Sea of Marrow by means of the Serpent Power. Passing the Middle Gate, it meets with the Jen Mo, or Channel of Function at the center of the brain (pineal gland) and descends the front of the body, returning to the center once more. Thus the flow of energy is a complete circle. When one reaches the extreme position, it comes back; returning is the movement of the Tao.

In this way the psychic centers are charged with energy which can then be circulated by means of the psychic channels and the magnetic field of their flow.

The Nei Ching also says, "Man possesses four seas and twelve meridians which are like rivers that flow to the ocean." The Sea of Nourishment represents the stomach. If there is too much energy, there is swelling of the abdomen; too little, and the patient cannot eat. The Sea of Blood is the meeting point of the twelve rivers. When there is excess, one feels heavy; when deficient, one feels uneasy. The Sea of Energy passes through the Gate of Jade, at the base of the skull; when it is affected one feels pain in the chest and presents a flushed expression, there is a sensation of breathlessness; when there is not enough energy, one cannot speak. Lastly, the Sea of Marrow. When it is overly full, one experiences an excess of energy; when it is empty, there are dizzy spells, tinnitus, pain in the calf muscle, and fainting.

Likewise, each organ stores the vital energy (except those that transform and transport). From these reservoirs, the Ninja may draw sufficient power in the form of Qi to perform what he wills. For example, in the demonstration of Tameshiwara—the breaking of bricks or stones with the bare hand—the Qi forms a protective glove, which prevents serious injury. Accomplishing such feats requires an understanding of the nature of energy as well as knowledge of how it circulates in the body.

The means whereby Qi may be "summoned" are few. All obey the laws of acupuncture. It is important to remember that one cannot truly "direct" the energy of the body; rather, by study and practice it is possible to establish a certain harmony by becoming attuned to the body's energy. This makes it possible to attain higher levels of consciousness. Then, and only then, if it is necessary, can one see the mysteries. If you know what to do, and how to do it, you can make the impossible seem commonplace.

DEER, CRANE, TURTLE

Probably the most ancient therapeutic exercises on record, from which all the other techniques described in this book are derived, are those of the Deer, Crane, and Turtle. These three exercises, which are done simultaneously, deal with the endocrine system, and must be performed first. Then the student will go on to the Longevity Exercises, which tone and strengthen the circulatory system, and finally the Da Mo Series, which stimulates the nervous system.

In seeking to coordinate and understand the various systems of the body, it is helpful to consider the modern analogy of telephone poles. Telephone poles may carry many types of lines: electrical, phone, cablevision. Yet while they run parallel, they do not interfere with one another. Furthermore, their major junctions and switching stations must necessarily be located in proximity to each other since they are travelling along similar paths. Likewise, the nerves, blood vessels, and even lymph glands, as well as their variety of trunks, operate in conjunction. Also, the phone lines carry their own mild charge of electricity, but cable lines must be powered at amplifiers along the route. The pattern for man evolves naturally, and is merely a macrocosm of how he himself unconsciously functions.

Also notice how three diverse systems—endocrine, circulatory, and nervous—are combined to create a physical manifestation, the human body, just as the triad of Yin (negative), Yang (positive), and Tao create balance. Such three-point symbolism is found in every major religion of the world—Father, Son, and Holy Ghost to the Christians; Shiva the Destroyer,

Shakti the Preserver, and Shanti the Arbiter in Hindu cosmology, and so on. In the Chinese system, which does not rely on subjugation to imaginary deities, these are expressed as the Void, which represents darkness and "No-Thing," into which light, the One-Point symbolized by the Third Eye or pineal gland, penetrated. And from the union of these two and their striving for balance, not domination as some people interpret them, arise all manifestations of the Universe.

Lao Tsu said it this way: "The nameless [void] is the beginning of Heaven and Earth. The named [light] is the mother of ten thousand things." So the pattern is now firmly established and historically documented, from the No-Thing to the One-Point to the Duality that their combination produces, for a total of three primary elemental sources for the Five Element classification system.

ORIGINS OF THE EXERCISES

Ancient Chinese legend states that wise men observed in Nature that the male deer (roebuck) was a most robust and virile animal. With powerful shoulders and springlike leaping ability, it ruled the forest and supported a harem of does. Its "manliness," if you will, found expression in the magnificent rack of antlers which was a crown of authority and rank in the wild. And the ancients contended that these antlers, which through the ages became a powerful symbol of male virility and were even thought to have aphrodisiacal powers, were generated as a consequence of "tail switching."

Seeking to emulate the buck, and thereby prolong life and sexual stamina, the ancients concluded that the almost constant brushing of the deer's tail against its genitals was responsible for a high level of reproductive hormones which kept it virile and aggressive. Thus, they believed, it was also desirable for a man to maintain the body in a state similar to that of late puberty, when young men are at the peak of physical endurance and energy—an age when they are often sent off to fight in foreign wars by kings who take advantage of their natural aggressive instincts.

It should be pointed out that deer horns on den walls were for some time a symbol of masculinity, in that they represented the tracking of the animal in its natural environment and killing it for food—the ancient tribal hunting ritual. And this implies a certain unconscious pact with Nature by the hunter, an understanding of his place in Nature and the Grand Cosmic Scheme. At this point in time, man is the top of the food chain. Nothing feeds on man, but man can eat everything. And so, historically, man has sought to establish a covenant with nature, so that he might be forgiven for having to take life to survive. From this belief, many primitive religions were born, for this is the natural order of things: "Great Fleas have little fleas, upon their backs to bite 'em; and little fleas have lesser fleas, and so ad infinitum."

Thus the Deer Exercise accesses one of the "base" emotions, or motivational drives, of the human. (The Deer Exercise for men, as described by Dr. Stephen Chang, has its counterpart in a similar exercise for women. The former stimulates the production of testosterone, while the latter causes the secretion of estrogen.) Most religions teach that this drive must be overcome or subdued in order to "see the face of God," reach Nirvana, or be enlightened. But the Chinese don't fight with themselves by suppressing these desires, or see the study of religion as a battle. Instead, through these exercises, they seek to establish a balance conducive to good health and longevity. One must therefore take care not to overdo the Deer Exercise in particular, lest one overstimulate oneself and become obnoxious. But the general rule of meditation is that it takes about one hundred days to see significant effects.

The exercises also require one to learn the essential and basic Bandhi, or muscle locks, as the Hindus call them, which are the foundation for control of the autonomic nervous system. The first is the anal lock, formed by tensing the bulbocavernosus muscle, which lies at the base of the torso with one loop constricting the anus and the other constricting the urethra, in order to prevent energy (Qi) leaking out of the body. This "lock" is accomplished by tightening the Hara or Tan T'ien, or squeezing the buttocks, as will be explained in the Crane Exercise.

The anal lock is the primary part of the Crane Exercise, but is performed in conjunction with the testicle cupping and belly rubbing of the Deer Exercise, and the raising and lowering of the head, which forms the main action of the Turtle Exercise.

Other such Bandhi include touching the roof of the mouth with the tip of the tongue to connect the two psychic channels on the front and back of the body. This is enhanced by dropping the chin to the chest to close the windpipe, the second Bandhi given in the exercises.

The anal lock promotes good digestion—and good health generally—by massaging the abdomen and large intestine. There are whole cults based on the therapeutic benefits of high colonic enemas. This exercise is mild by comparison, but it should still not be taken to extremes. One should never strain; meditation is an art of relaxation and patience.

One must have a tight rein on the mind not to succumb to the lure of physical and sensual pleasure induced by the release of high levels of hormonal activators provoked by this exercise.

But is this not the very promise of all transcendental practice, to rise above the carnal desires of the lower chakras and ascend to that lofty plane of Cosmic Consciousness and Universal Mind? Certainly, one must be of high moral character even to begin such a quest, lest one fall victim to desire and come under the spell of what the ancients called the Fox Spirit, and which the Greeks knew as Succubus, a creature of the Id, who entices one to perversion.

The ancients were not unaware of these aspects of the practice, and so have provided countermeasures to facilitate the proper mental attitude. First, concentration is required to keep the mind on the goal of meditation and lift it above the physical plane. Second, should an erection occur due to tactile stimulation, they advise placing the thumb of the hand cupping the testicles at the base of the penis next to the pubis and pressing down sharply. This will inhibit the flow of blood into the penis (preventing erection) and maximize the buildup of energy within the sexual glands. Is it any wonder that the masters chose their students carefully and couched their teaching in ambiguous and obscure terminology?

This brings up yet another occult teaching, namely that many esoteric terms have a double or coded meaning. The bulbocavernosus muscle exercised by the anal lock Bandhi in the Crane Exercise, for example, is shaped like a figure eight. It should be noted that the figure eight, two concentric loops crossing at their apex, has long been a symbol of Immortality among the mystics who sought to turn lead into gold. Is it not possible that the ancient hermits who conjured up the mystic lore provided this clue to the practice of therapeutic postures and exercises designed to promote good health and longevity, the very foundation of which is the meditative practices spoken of thus far? How else could an ancient physician, being discouraged by religious taboos from conducting autopsies or cadaver dissection, discover the shape of that fundamental muscle, so essential to Qi Gong practice, except by means of the Inner Quest? Or even that it could be mentally controlled by concentrating on an imaginary spot on the smooth sheet of the lower abdominal wall?

As one text describes it, "the secrets of meditative skill would make a grown man blush and a woman giggle," since they deal with sexual functions as well. Not only is this encoded, but also much of the direct formulation is given in allegorical terms. This was as much to protect the delicate nature of the teachings as it was to confuse those who would misuse or pervert them. Furthermore, so many of the early Chinese ideograms, like the aged Egyptian hieroglyphs, could be read more than one way, and their meanings have become lost and blurred with the passage of time and the interpretation of scholars more distantly removed from the Source.

Thus, while one might read a medieval alchemical formula as the transmutation of base metals into valuable ones, the true student will translate lead, mercury, and gold into Body, Mind, and Spirit, and realize that the secret of longevity is good health, and the secret of good health is control of the body through the endocrine glands—the system accessed by the Deer, Crane, and Turtle Exercises.

The first of these glands, and the one which is acted upon by the regulation of breathing and the constriction of the bulbocavernosus muscle, is the prostate. It is located directly under the center of the figure eight muscle, and controls sexual desire. It is the transmutation of this primitive urge into the higher principles of moral conduct that is the work of the Yogi and the Ninja. That is what the hidden masters meant, not that one should smelt quicksilver into precious metals and thereby become rich so as to enjoy life—for what is all the wealth of the world, if one is in poor health? No, they meant to transform the Self into a Being who could enjoy the fullness of life because of his extreme good health and longevity. Many of the ancient sages are renowned for their acrobatic exploits and sexual prowess. Master Li Ch'ing Yuen, who died in 1921, was said to be over two hundred years old, yet he was active and agile until his death and married fourteen times, living to see 180 descendants, spanning eleven generations.

The Hara

A second part of the Deer Exercise focuses on the center of spiritual and physical well-being: the Hara. This is a Japanese word from the martial art called Aikido, which is taken to mean "center" or One-Point. Located about two inches below the navel on the centerline of the body, it is the physical, geographic center of gravity of the human body. This is true regardless of size, obesity, or physical deformity. Tai Chi Chuan players, Aikidoists, and other martial artists focus their attention on this spot when training to develop "waist balance," which provides them with surer footing in combat. So, too, do the Ninja.

Modern, or distantly removed, martial arts may neglect this basic facet of training or even dispense with meditative practice altogether, thinking it too cerebral to be of value to a fighting man. Or the scholar who dislikes drill will avoid it owing to its repetitive nature. But both must eventually learn this lesson of body dynamics, the one by steady practice of technique and the other through directed mental concentration.

The Hara in Chinese medicine is known as the Golden Stove. It is the first of the Three Burning Spaces that make up the Triple Warmer Meridian of acupuncture. In meditation its symbol is a red ruby. It is here where Air will be "cooked" and the Qi, or Life Force, will be extracted and purified to nourish the body.

To prevent the loss of vital energy from the body, various "channels" and "gates" must be opened or arranged to circulate within a closed orbit. To this end is formed the first mudra, or Finger Knitting Position, in which the fingers are closed around the thumbs of each hand. (See p. 46 for more details.)

While the Outer Gates—the eyes, ears, nose, and mouth—are closed by lowering the lids and placing the tongue against the palate, the Inner Gates are opened up along the spine, or Heavenly Pillar, to permit the internal circulation of energy known as the Microcosmic Orbit. The anal and urethral openings are also closed by constriction of the bulbocavernosus muscle, which extends across the floor of the pelvis, to prevent loss of energy. Therefore, to control this cosmic energy one need only alter the rate of respiration, which will adjust the pH of the blood and produce a relaxed meditative state in which the energy may be observed and regulated.

To accomplish this, the ancients have taught that there are two basic methods: natural, like that used in the harmonizing breath, wherein the Hara expands with inhalation and compresses on exhalation; and reverse breathing, in which the Hara contracts when inhaling and expands when exhaling. Each has its functions and uses. Beyond this is the consideration of the four steps in breathing: inhaling, holding the inhalation, exhaling, and holding the exhalation. The interval of each of these phases may also be altered to various ends. And it should be observed that they correspond to the phases of the circulation of Yang to Yin described in the Sky to Ground explanation.

Once learned, synchronize inhalation and exhalation with the expansion and contraction of the abdomen and the tensing and relaxation of the anal lock. This will enhance the performance and benefits of both exercises. Observe that the instructions for these exercises are almost identical with those for natural breathing, albeit infinitely more detailed.

The best time to practice the Crane and Deer forms is in the morning, while facing the sun if possible, because the sun represents life and positive energy (Yang) and increases the mental imagery of drawing in warmth and light that can heal and rejuvenate the body. Begin by performing no more than three repetitions, and build up to twelve. Mentally repeat some simple phrase such as, "In comes the good air; out goes the bad air," to program the subconscious with positive thoughts and remove the toxins and stale air from the lungs. But say no more than nine words at a time.

One may also wish to practice before retiring. In that case, face north at midnight. This tones the inner organs and relaxes the body for sleep. But note: Women should abstain from this during pregnancy.

Male Deer Exercises

Begin by rubbing the palms of the hands together vigorously. This creates heat in the hands and brings the energy of the body into the palms and fingers. With the right hand, cup the testicles inside the hand so that the palm covers the scrotum. (The best way to perform this exercise is naked.) Do not squeeze; just a light pressure should be felt, as well as heat from the hand going into the testicles. Place the palm of the left hand on the area of the pubis, one inch below the navel. Rotate the hand counterclockwise eighty-one times ($9 \times 9 = 81$, Shugendo) with slight pressure so a gentle warmth begins to build up in the pubis area. Then reverse the hands (to balance the energy), making sure to vigorously rub the palms together to generate heat, and rub in the opposite direction eighty-one times. (In Taoism, the number of Yang, or high positive energy, is nine. Hence, $9 \times 9 = 81$, or the highest possible Yang energy. So one rubs eighty-one times in this pose.)

After completing the part of the exercise with each hand, tighten the muscles surrounding the anal opening. This is accomplished by fixing on the Hara. When properly done, a pleasant feeling will travel from the base of the spine to the top of the head. This is due to pressure being placed on the prostate gland as it is gently massaged by the action of closing the anal muscles. The sexual energy is thus diverted up the glandular system into the top of the head and to the pineal gland. In Taoist Yoga, this process is known as Kindling the Fire, Refining the Qi, Ascent of the Positive Fire up the Heavenly Pillar (called Awakening of the Kundalini Serpent Power in Hatha Yoga), and the opening of the Thousand Petal Lotus (enlightenment in Ch'an Buddhism.)

Male-Deer Exercise: Hand Warming Place one hand atop the other and rotate in a circular manner; reverse top and bottom, and circle in the opposite direction an equal number of times; or place the palms together and rub back and forth vigorously to warm the palms and stimulate the flow of Qi from the solar plexus through the Yin and Yang Yu Channels of the arms to the Tiger Center in the right palm and the Dragon Center in the left. This feeling of warmth and of relaxation in the hands is the first step in recognizing the flow of Qi, the Life Force, within the body. The number of repetitions may be of no real significance, but in internal alchemy, twenty-four of each is to be performed. This is explained symbolically in that 6 is the number of delusion while 4 is that of the alchemical elements (6 × 4 = 24).

Hand Warming   **Hara**

Male Deer Exercise: The Hara   Wrap the fingers of the right hand around the thumb so that the energy generated by the hand rubbing exercise is not lost, and stand the fist on the knee. Symbolically, this represents occult, or "hidden," knowledge and is a socially acceptable alternative to cupping the testicles. Place the left, open palm on the Hara, or "center," a point two inches below the navel, and rub in a circular motion with gentle pressure eighty-one times. Reverse the hands and repeat. The number of repetitions is determined by the number 9, the number of completion, which is derived from the number of Yin, Yang, and Tao: 3. $3 \times 3 = 9$; $9 \times 9 = 81$. The Hara is the center of physical and spiritual well-being. If this area is warm, one is halfway to Immortality.

Female Deer Exercise

The female deer exercise is as follows, once again according to Dr. Stephen Chang, from his excellent work *The Book of Internal Exercises:*

> Sit so that you can bring the heel of one foot so that it presses into and up against the opening of the vagina. You will want a steady and fairly hard pressure from the heel into the vagina, so that the heel presses tightly against the clitoris. You may experience a pleasant sensation due to the stimulation of the genital area and a subsequent release of sexual energy.
>
> Begin by rubbing the hands vigorously. Place the hands on the breasts so that you can feel the heat from the hands enter the skin. Now rub with the hands in an outward, circular manner. (Right hand counterclockwise, left hand clockwise.) Perform this motion a minimum of 36 times and a maximum of 306 times. This outward circular motion is called dispersion, and helps to prevent or cure lumps and cancer of the breasts. One should also reverse the motion of the hands to an inward rubbing motion an equal number of times. This is called stimulation, and its effect is to enlarge the breasts.

You will feel a warmth or fire building in the breasts and/or the genital region. This assures that the sexual energy is building within the body.

After finishing this part of the Deer Exercise, tighten the muscles of the vagina and anus, as if trying to close both openings. You may feel a pleasant sensation rising to the top of the head. As with all Taoist exercises, you do not want to force this action.

In both cases, when the anal lock is learned it should be done in conjunction with the massage of the Hara or breasts. The effects of this are many. It prevents and cures hemorrhoids, prevents vaginal infections and colitis, and strengthens the sexual organs.

Women are cautioned against practicing the Deer Exercise during menses, as this may enhance the experience. Neither should it be performed during pregnancy, since this increased stimulation of the glands may induce premature labor. Some women may find the menstrual cycle reduced in intensity, or cease altogether from this practice.

Crane Exercises

The crane has long been held as a symbol of longevity in China, but few know the reason why. The first scientists, observers of life and Nature, noticed that the stately crane was possessed of great balance and seemed never to suffer gastrointestinal distress. They reasoned that this was due to the frequent massage the bird gave itself in the abdominal area by standing on one leg and pressing against the belly with the folded limb. Either that, or someone figured out that increased abdominal motility could be obtained by judicious massage, and pointed to the crane as an example which proved the theory (or at least demonstrated the technique required). In any event, the practice of the exercise improves digestion, and therefore nutrition, circulation, and immune response.

This exercise cures a multitude of ailments common to modern man with his high sodium, high cholesterol diet:

constipation, diarrhea, ulcers, diverticulitis, and cancers of the
stomach, intestine, and colon. In one of the advanced techniques of Hatha Yoga, the entire digestive system below the
diaphragm is massaged by performing the Abdominal Lift:
squeezing the lower torso against the spine and rolling the
belly vigorously.

This pose may be practiced standing, sitting, or prone.
Begin by rubbing the hands together vigorously. Then place the
hands, palms down, on the lower abdomen. Men place the
thumb of the left hand in the navel and cover the left hand with
the right; women press the navel with the right thumb and
cover the right hand with the left. Now begin to exhale slowly,
and at the same time press the hands down lightly so that the
abdomen forms a hollow cavity. This motion forces the air out
of the abdomen and lower lungs. (The Yoga tradition divides
Air into *pana* and *apana*: that which is expelled from the upper
body and that which is expelled from the bowels.) In this
instance, the hands are like the leg of the crane. After you
exhale completely, begin to inhale slowly and extend the
abdomen outward so that it becomes like a balloon. Try not to
allow your chest to expand—you want to use only the muscles
of the lower abdomen while breathing. With continued practice, you will be able to expand and contract the abdomen quite
easily. In the beginning, the hands act as guides. Once mastered, however, the pose does not require them.

Crane Exercise: Tan T'ien   Tan T'ien is the Chinese term for
the "center," or One-Point. Now that the area of the lower
abdomen is warmed, this exercise is used to focus the concentration on the Inner Self. Medicinally, it is used to cure
ailments of the digestive tract. Many diseases are prevented
and cured by this exercise. Contract the sphincter muscles of
the colon as in the Yogic Moola Bandhi, or anal lock. Place the
palms of both hands against the lower belly and exhale completely. Use gentle pressure against the Hara to empty the
"lower lungs" fully. Inhale slowly and deeply, filling the lungs
from bottom to top, like water as it pours into a glass. As the
lungs expand, the belly will inflate, raising the hands as the

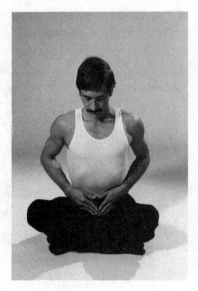

Tan T'ien

vital Life Force is drawn into the "seat of breathing." Repeat twelve times.

Turtle Exercises

All of the vertebrae must be properly aligned if the Serpent Power is to rush up the spine and flood the brain; and the neck area is filled with the trunk-line nerves that feed the rest of the body. The Turtle Exercise massages and aligns the vertebrae of the cervical region.

The Turtle Exercise stretches the entire spine, energizes the neck, strengthens the shoulder muscles, and removes stiffness, soreness and tiredness from the neck and shoulders. In addition, it stimulates the thyroid and parathyroid glands, improving the metabolism.

Begin by bringing the chin down into the chest and stretching the top of the head upward. (Touching the chin to the chest at the site of the jugular notch between the collarbones is another Yogic Bandhi—this time to seal the windpipe.) The

Bowing   **Yielding**

back of the neck will feel a stretch upward and the shoulders will relax downward. Then slowly bring the back of the skull down as if to touch it to the back of the neck. The chin will point upward, and the throat will be slightly stretched. The shoulders will now pull upward on either side of the head as if you were trying to touch them to the ears. These two movements imitate the tortoise, for whom the exercise is named.

Synchronize the movements of the head with Crane Breathing and the Deer Exercise. As you lower the chin to the chest, inhale. Exhale as you lift the chin to the sky. Tipping the head forward is called bowing, which lowers the blood pressure. Tipping the head backward raises the blood pressure; it is called yielding. Notice how this corresponds to the action of Yang energy, descending from above, displacing the Yin which ascends from below. Indeed, does not a bull lower its head to charge, an aggressive masculine gesture, while the horse jerks its head backward to escape danger, a retreating, defensive movement? Always observe the pattern of Nature and its infinite variety.

Turtle Exercise: Bowing   Close the fingers of both hands around the thumbs to prevent the loss of energy thus far accumulated. On the final movement of the previous posture, all of the air will have been expelled from the lungs and the lower abdomen; then begin this exercise by dropping the chin to the chest. This stretches the muscles of the neck, thereby stimulating the nerves which lead from the brain to the rest of the body. As the head is tilted forward the shoulders relax downward, thus helping to relieve tension and stress in that area. Practice of this form prevents many headaches, especially those due to unconscious tensing of the shoulder girdle while working. Maintain a feeling of warmth and relaxation in the Hara using the sacral lock, and let the Qi energy circulate in the Center as you perform the described chin lock, known in Yoga as the Jalandhara Bandhi.

Turtle Exercise: Yielding   Tilt the head as far back as comfortably possible. Do not strain or overexert, simply let the head loll back and relax. Inhale slowly and deeply through the nose, filling the lungs from bottom to top with fresh, clean air. As the head tips backward, the shoulders will rise slightly and the chest will expand naturally. Tilting the head forward lowers the blood pressure; tipping it back raises the blood pressure. When used in combination, they pump freshly oxygenated blood to the brain and maintain flexibility of the cervical vertebrae. By releasing the sacral lock as the head is laid back, the feeling of warmth in the Hara can be felt to rush up the spine and flood the brain with energy.

Twelve repetitions of this combination exercise of Deer-Crane-and-Turtle per session are generally sufficient for maintaining good health. Again, use the fingers-around-thumb mudra or Kuji Kiri to close the fists. (Kuji Kiri is explained in greater detail in the section beginning on p. 65.)

LI CH'ING YUEN'S LONGEVITY EXERCISES: PART ONE

As indicated in the previous section, the Deer, Crane, and Turtle exercises are the foundation of all meditative practice and from them arise virtually every exercise in Chinese Qi Gong and Hindu Yoga. In this section we will explore the therapeutic movements that open the channels, gates, and meridians of the circulation of the vital Life Force, Qi, within the physical body.

These exercises are known by many names: the Longevity Exercise of Li Ch'ing Yuen, the Eight Pieces of Brocade, Silk Weaving Exercise, and many others, depending on which school of breath control one may be attending. In India, for instance, in deference to Hatha (Sun and Moon) Yoga, all the breathing techniques are known collectively as Pranayama, "prana" being the term used to define what the Chinese call Qi, and "yama" meaning control, or circulation, of the same. At more advanced levels, the techniques for cultivating the refined essence are referred to as Raja Yoga, the arts reserved for the princes, or raja.

These, like those of Qi Gong, were withheld from the large mass of the population. This was partly due to the mistaken impression by those who elect themselves to be the few who rule that the many who serve were not capable, nor had they the time, to develop these skills.

In ancient times, the sages of China and the gurus of India, having learned these inner mysteries, would travel about the countryside searching for a kingdom in which the people were already healthy, happy, and well fed—indications that the ruler was both kind and benevolent. There they would approach the royal court and offer to teach the king the secrets of Immortality so that his domain could continue to prosper and flourish.

As the leaders saw fit and necessary, many of the benefits of these exercises were passed on to the general population, and some, like the Iron Body, found their way into the military disciplines that protected the kingdom. After all, most of the economy of those times was agricultural or depended on accommodating the trade routes, so there was little need for a farmer to develop an Iron Body, but quite advantageous for the palace guards and those who protected the caravans to have such ability. (Bear in mind that the Iron Body cannot be achieved until one has balanced the internal energy, which above all leads to good health.)

These exercises are the starting point. They are designed and intended to be done upon rising in the morning and before bed at night to insure proper functioning of the internal organs, as well as to develop a calm mind in a healthy body. They are performed sitting, with very little movement but great emphasis on breath. Therefore, they can be used to enter a meditative state of complete relaxation where hypnotic (external) or auto-suggestive (internal) directions may be given and accepted for whatever purpose the practitioner may desire.

It goes without saying that such "suggestions" should be of a positive, life-affirming nature and as uncomplicated as possible for easy assimilation and direction along the True Path. Destructive commands or intentions usually bring about poor results or internal imbalances of energy that result in one simply losing interest, or, in worst case scenarios, becoming physically ill. Just do the exercise. When you understand why you wanted to hit someone or take revenge, the desire for it will drop away and both of you will be better for it.

Li Ch'ing Yuen was a Chinese herbalist who, according to legend, lived to be well over 250 years old. He accomplished this amazing feat by performing these exercises every day for 120 years.

That he actually lived is well documented in Oriental history. He is said to have married fourteen times, and lived to see over 180 sons, daughters, and grandchildren. He could walk very quickly and had good eyesight even in his later years. He was photographed toward the and of his days and was such a symbol of reverence that a picture of him was presented to Gen. Chiang Kai-shek. The *New York Times* reported his passing in 1930.

His great longevity is not considered extraordinary among those who practice such therapeutic movements; it is merely proof that the techniques work.

THE SIX EXERCISES

Technically speaking, the Longevity Exercises of Li Ch'ing Yuen consist of the Cranial Pump, Nine Deep Breaths, Beating the Heavenly Drum, Twisting the Heavenly Pillar, Juice of Jade, and Kindling the Fire (warming and massaging the kidneys). This brings the student to a relaxed state of contemplation, at which point the breathing exercises are performed. The Six Healing Breaths is only one exercise that may be done at this point; the student will find this and others in the Inner Journey section beginning on p. 60.

At the conclusion of the Qi Gong—the breathing exercise— one must "return to the world" by slowly beginning to rouse oneself from the deep contemplative state. To accomplish this, one begins with the exercise Turning the Wheel, then by stretching out the legs to perform Two Hands Uphold the Sky, and concluding with Leaning Forward and Touching the Toes, for a total of eight movements, hence they are sometimes referred to as the Eight Brocade Pieces.

Other self-massage and channeling of energy exercises given in this section are therapeutic and medicinal in nature, and serve to correct any imbalances of Qi that may be present in the body due to the stress of everyday life or illness.

These exercises were already popular during the time of Master Li. They are described in old Taoist texts on Immortality, and several books have been written about them in recent years, as they are enjoying a revival of interest in the modern era.

Health and fitness are always worthwhile goals, and the work of attaining them may begin at any time, since they require a lifetime of maintenance. The effects of practice are cumulative and cannot be seen in a single day. Perseverance is a must, but each time the exercises are performed they become easier. After a while one may find that an old injury or minor soreness may feel better; when this happens one knows the exercises are working.

They are most effective if done twice a day, upon waking— before noon—and before going to bed—between the hours of 11 P.M. and 1 A.M. It takes about twenty minutes to perform one set. Do not overexert or do more than the required number of repetitions. And never use force or strain; the goal is relaxation.

The Cranial Pump

Turn the palms upward and wrap the fingers around the thumbs. Close the eyes and place the tip of the tongue against the roof of the mouth. Click your teeth together lightly, at a

Cranial Pump

slow, even pace, or clench the jaw muscles tightly thirty-six times. This exercise can calm the fever of the heart. It also promotes strong healthy teeth and gums by stimulating the roots. The clicking causes vibrations, which resonate through the bones of the skull to stimulate and clear the brain. Teeth clicking or jaw clenching also moves the tongue against the roof of the mouth. This exerts a slight pressure against the palate, which stimulates the pineal gland—the master gland of the endocrine system—located deep inside the brain. Just as the Sacral Pump, as practiced in the Deer, Crane, and Turtle exercises, lifts the energy from the lower Tan T'ien (Hara) to the heart, which in turn raises it to the middle Tan T'ien, the Cranial Pump elevates it to the brain.

The Nine Deep Breaths

Place the hands over the ears and press gently. This will warm them and benefit the kidneys. Then inhale, drawing air into the Hara, and exhale, letting it rise up the back to the head. Breathe so slowly and deeply—nine times—that you cannot hear the

Nine Deep Breaths   **Heavenly Pillar**

sound of your respiration. If the mind is calm, one can hear the heart beating. With the hands in place, tap the base of the skull with the index fingers forty-eight times, twenty-four on each side by alternating the fingers. This prevents and cures deafness by stimulating circulation to the ears, as well as calming the mind. Another name for this exercise is Beating the Heavenly Drum.

The Heavenly Pillar

In Chinese medicine, the head, neck, and back compose the Heavenly Pillar, which supports the temple of the body, which houses the spirit. Placing your hands on your knees, turn your head and shoulders slowly to the left while exhaling. Inhale as you return to the center and exhale while turning to the right. Repeat twenty-four times in each direction for a total of forty-eight, looking as far to the rear as is comfortable on each half rotation. This exercise opens the Nine Gates of the spine so that Qi, or Chi (the old form of spelling), may rise from the lower Tan T'ien to the Mysterious Chamber of the head. It tones and stimulates the entire body, prevents many illnesses, and improves posture.

The Juice of Jade

The tongue is the "finger of the mind." With it we express all our thoughts, hopes, and fears. In the alchemical practice of immortality it is known by its Chinese medical name, the Red Dragon. In this exercise it is used to clean and massage the gums and teeth. With eyes closed and hands resting on knees, run the tip of the tongue around the inside of the teeth from left to right eighteen times. Reverse, circling inside from right to left eighteen times. Repeat, running the tongue around the outside of the teeth in the same manner. Swish the saliva back and forth from the tip to the root of the tongue thirty-six times. This is the Juice of Jade, which promotes good health by improving the absorption and circulation of nutrients from food by stimulating the production of digestive enzymes in saliva. Divide the liquid into three parts (representing Heaven,

Juice of Jade

Earth, and Man) and swallow each with a vigorous gulp. This exercise also stimulates the flow of digestive enzymes, thereby promoting better digestion and absorption of nutrients.

Kindling the Fire

Warm the hands by rubbing them as before and place them on the back just over the kidneys. Massage lightly in an upward and outward direction twenty-four times. Lean forward slightly and hold the hands over the kidneys for a few minutes, letting them absorb the warmth of the palms. The kidneys filter and purify the blood and are vital to the immune system. This exercise cures and prevents many illnesses of the urinary tract. In alchemy, this is called "kindling the fire" to "boil the juice of jade" in the "golden stove" of the lower Tan T'ien so that it may rise like steam up the "heavenly pillar" to the "mysterious chamber" where lives the "higher Self," teacher of the warrior way of enlightenment and keeper of the "golden elixir" (refined oxygen-rich blood) of Immortality.

Kindling the Fire   The Primordial Breath

The Primordial Breath

Man can live for many days without food and a few days
without water, but not even a few minutes without air. Therefore, the art of regulating the breath is most important. With
eyes closed, fingers around thumbs and hands on knees, back
straight and tip of tongue on roof of mouth, inhale slowly and
deeply, drawing the breath deep into the lungs from bottom to
top, but not overfilling. Tighten the seat muscles (anal or sacral
lock), clench the fists around the thumbs (heart pump), tilt the
chin down (chin lock), and hold the breath with the diaphragm
(not the throat) for as long as you can without strain. (It is said if
one can maintain this for one hundred heartbeats one will need
neither doctors nor medicine.) Relax and let the air out through
the mouth as when sighing, letting all negative thoughts and
impurities be carried away, dispelled in relaxation. Feel the
warmth and relaxation as it flows over the body, healing and
restoring vitality to every fiber of the being.

Now one is prepared for the Six Healing Breaths and the
Inner Journey of meditation.

THE INNER JOURNEY

Whosoever shall descend the Crater of Sneffels Jocule touched by the peak shadow at the vernal equinox will come to the center of the earth.
    I have done it.
                            —Jules Verne, from *Journey to the Center of the Earth* (1870)

The Ninja have long recognized that nourishment must be transported to every cell of the human body for life to be sustained, and that health is a matter of maintaining a proper balance among the various elements. Illness, it then follows, must be the result of an imbalance of this energy.

Various systems may be used to manipulate this balance, to adjust and restore it should it be affected by extremes of heat and cold, injury or disease of any sort. Acupuncture is one type of Chinese medicine. It has developed from the much more subtle art of massage, which, in turn, came from meditation and knowledge of Self. Qi Gong is another method: hyper- and hypoventilation which alters the pH of the blood. While massage is essentially hydraulic in nature, Qi Gong is more chemical. Acupuncture is, of course, nervous and electrical.

The goal of meditation, it will be recalled, is the symbolic uniting of the Yang pole atop the head and the Yin on the perineum. Meditation not only provides visual, audible, and tactile cues to enforce this concept, but operates by all of the above means.

This is the point in the sequence of exercises at which real meditation begins. The body, having been relaxed by the first movements of the Longevity Series, is now prepared to circulate the Qi extracted from the air through the breath. The Heavenly Pillar has been aligned, the Jade Gate (at the base of the skull) opened, and the breath has been slowed. One is now ready to experience the inner energy.

THE INNER ENERGY OF QI

The first step is purification. This is accomplished by the Six Healing Breaths. Next, the Qi will be raised to the Mysterious Chamber, the skull, by lifting it up the Nine Steps of the Heavenly Pillar using the nine Kuji Kiri finger-knitting exercises.

The Six Healing Breaths

The Six Healing Breaths are a method of purifying and removing impurities from the twelve organs of the body. These will be explained and the relationships of solid to empty, Yin to Yang, given elsewhere. For the present, it is sufficient to state the organs are divided into the Five Elements, or categories, which correspond both to the fingers and to the five basic colors. This is an excellent exercise with which to conclude a meditation, since it harmonizes and balances the energy of the body. Further it helps to prevent and cure many illnesses. Each breath and its accompanying sound should be repeated three to six times.

One begins by focusing on the liver. Inhale slowly and deeply, filling the liver on the right side of the ribs with healing cleansing air. This also stimulates the associated organ, the gall bladder. Both are of the element Wood.

Exhale slowly and completely, whispering the sound "shu" (pronounced like "shoe") while visualizing a green mist being expelled from the lips, and with it all impurities from the liver. After three to six repetitions, rub the left thumb with the index finger and thumb of the right hand. Then twist it gently a few times, and give a gentle tug. Repeat with the right thumb.

Inhale slowly and deeply into the solar plexus. This is the breath of the heart and small intestine, Fire elements. Fill the heart with pure, fresh energy. Exhale, whispering the syllable "haa" and imagining a red mist being expelled. Repeat three times. Then massage, twist, and tug the middle finger of the left hand, then the right.

Inhale deeply into the stomach and spleen on the left side of the ribcage. Again, absorb healing and purifying energy into the organ, then exhale, whispering the sound "huu" (pronounced like "who") to push a yellow mist from the system. This set of paired organs is of the Earth element. Do this three to six times, then stroke, turn, and pull the left pinky finger, then the right.

Draw a deep healing breath into the lungs, filling them completely. The lungs are related to the element Air and to the large intestine. Then exhale a white mist saying the word "ssh" (as if quieting an infant) at least three times, to cleanse impurities from the lungs. Then massage the index fingers, left then right, as before.

Take a deep breath and draw it into the kidneys. Lean slightly forward for this exercise. The kidneys and bladder are related to the Water element. Exhale, whispering the sound "chway" (pronounced "ch–way," with a long "a" sound) and seeing a gray mist being issued from the body. Repeat three to six times, then massage the ring fingers of both hands as before, left first.

Lastly, draw clean fresh air into the "triple warmer," or "three burning spaces," an organ unknown to Western medicine, represented by the Hara, solar plexus, and the Third Eye. These are the three cauldrons of alchemical terminology. The Triple Warmer is associated with the Circulation-Sex Meridian of acupuncture, generally believed to be the pericardium and the state of the blood vessels. It is also, like the heart, associated with the Fire element. The sound to be whispered on exhalation is "she." The expelled mist should be seen as orange. Again, do this three to six times.

For this sixth breath, the finger-rubbing practice consists of rubbing the palms together, then hooking the fingers, not interlacing them, with right above left, and pulling so that the action stretches the wrists, elbows, and shoulder joints. Then reverse, with the left on top, and again pull gently.

Women, being of Yin nature, should perform the Six Healing Breaths in reverse order: liver, triple warmer, kidneys, lungs, spleen, and heart.

The Healing Breaths may be performed twice per day. Again, do no less than three nor more than six repetitions, including the finger massage, per set. (Note that the finger rubbing exercises are a prelude to Kuji Kiri mudras discussed later in this section, and serve to draw the Qi to the palms so it can be connected through those exercises.)

The Fourfold Breath

The Six Healing Breaths in the previous section are the mantras, sounds, or "words of power" in some of the darker cults. Each vibrates at a particular frequency, which sets up a resonance in the associated organ, cleansing and purifying it by expelling all negative thoughts, emotions, or energy. Each of these may be directed at an adversary, depending on which sort of elemental energy is required to overcome him.

If the enemy is angry, for example, he is expressing the emotion of Fire. In the elemental relationships, Water destroys Fire. So if the enemy is screaming "Haa!" as he charges forward, he can be stopped by "Shhh," the sound of the Water element, which dispels fear, the cause of anger.

The principle at work here is to restore his balance. The Ninja, of course, balances his energy with the Six Sounds Exercise (the Six Healing Breaths) and by proper breathing. This enables him to perceive the imbalance in others and himself, and to heal them, and himself.

The breathing exercise whereby this is accomplished is called the Fourfold Breath, and is performed after the purifying ritual of the Six Healing Breaths. This rhythm of breathing should be continued throughout the remainder of the exercises.

The purpose of the exercises in this book is to calm the "lower self," the chakras, or energy centers of the body, which are concerned only with gratification of the physical desires—

air, water, food, shelter, and sex. In so doing, the energy of the body can be raised and with it the level of consciousness. When this has been accomplished, we are sensitive to the forces of Nature and can act in accordance with the laws of the Universe.

One need only begin. It may require more effort for some than others, and it may need to be attempted several times, even at different ages, to effect a sufficient rapport with this alter ego, but it can be done. It has before and will again.

Much nonsense has been written and spoken concerning breathing exercises. They have been condemned as dangerous, they have been lauded as miraculous; and they have been wrenched from the context of the systems to which they belong and, inevitably, been misused. We shall consider one form of breathing exercise which is linked to the practice of relaxation on the one hand, as well the intake of the psychic energy and etheric vitality known in Yoga as *prana*. This is, if carried out as described here, perfectly safe.

Here we must point out an important part of the technique. In doing the exercise, the student is required to hold the breath for a stated time. Most people attempt to accomplish this by closing the throat and nasal passages by an effort of will. As far as these breathing exercises are concerned, such a method is DANGEROUS and should *never be attempted*. It is because of this that many people run into trouble.

The correct method of retaining the breath is to breathe in for the allotted period, allowing the chest muscles and the great diaphragm muscle which lies between the chest and the intestinal area to expand the chest and so fill the lungs with air. The chest should now be *held expanded*, and the diaphragm muscle *held down*. The lungs are now full of air, and this is being retained. But—and this is the test—if the chest is tapped sharply the air should be partly expelled; there should be no barrier in the throat or mouth. This way of retaining the breath does not throw any strain upon the lung tissue, which is one of the chief dangers of any such exercise. If this procedure is correctly carried out, there is no physical danger at all. In fact, since most people use only a fraction of the total lung area at their disposal, and some with certain cases of neuroses use even less than the average, an exercise which carefully engages more of the lungs' capacity can be extremely beneficial.

The most useful of the breathing exercises for general use is the Fourfold Breath.

Sit or lie in a relaxed condition and breathe in the following way:

1. Inhale slowly, mentally counting one, two, three, four. Now hold the breath, counting one, two.
2. Exhale at the same speed, again counting one, two, three, four. Now hold the lungs empty without movement, counting one, two.

Repeat this cycle for about five minutes, not longer, at the commencement of the practice. Later on the time may be extended.

It is important that until the student is thoroughly proficient in this basic technique of relaxation and in the Fourfold Breath, he should not attempt the other techniques given herein. This involves work, but without this the greater work may not be done, nor the goal of an Iron Body achieved.

Kuji Kiri

Kuji Kiri are the finger-knitting positions—called mudras in the Hindu and Tibetan traditions—used in Ninjitsu to elevate the Qi, the Life Force, collected, cultivated, and refined in the lower Tan T'ien, from the base of the spine to the pineal gland in the center of the brain.

This is done in a particular sequence so that this energy is raised progressively from one "gate" to another up the Heavenly Pillar (spine). It will be recalled from the Map of the Body that there are nine such gates. The primary three are the coccyx (sacral pump), heart (middle pump), and skull (cranial pump), represented in the Juice of Jade as Heaven, Earth, and Man. Each of these primary centers of energy, or gates, are held to be sites where Qi can be collected and circulated into a vortex, which sets the next gate spinning in the opposite direction, much like interlocking gears.

Between each primary gate are two lesser gates, so each one of the three is composed of three. For example, the first three are associated with food, shelter, and sex—the three primal urges of man—back to the Juice of Jade again, and so on for the other two, making a total of nine. From this it can be seen that the Ninja were not only consistent in their symbolism and explanation, but poetic as well.

These "associated motivations," or primal drives, then form a part of the philosophical basis for many of the spiritual teachings, and moral and ethical codes, which govern the social interaction of the individual, clan, and nation. It is obviously easier to be kind, gentle, and caring when one has a secure supply of food, shelter from the elements, and a loving mate. So, "raising" the Qi from the Golden Stove is also an analogy for "elevating the consciousness" to a higher level. The Hindu version of this is known as "overcoming the lower chakras," the base desires that, although necessary for survival, often contribute to conflict.

Naturally, the "emotion" associated with the heart is compassion and reverence for all life. And the two lesser centers represent similar emotive responses like empathy and mercy, while the upper three, crowned by the Third Eye, represent levels of intellectual comprehension.

These then—the Nine Gates, the Nine Finger-Knits, and the Nine Emotional Responses—represent the Nine Levels of Power. For as the student experiences each of them in sequence, he gains mental control over his emotions and intellect, enabling him to retain his balance in the face of the world's absurdity, created by those who do not yet, or will not, understand. Remember, that although we are dealing with the psychological and philosophical underpinnings of both society and religion, we are *not* "changing" anyone's religious or moral code with these exercises. That is the meaning in Shugendo that "nine retains its own identity."

Some hold that the *mudras* are methods of connecting the various acupuncture points in the hands to create "circuits" of energy for a specific purpose. Others believe that Qi is more like the electromagnetic field that surrounds a wire, and it is the proximity of these "fields" that produces an effect, in which case any relative juxtaposition of the hands would suffice. Still others feel that these are merely mnemonic devices used to program the body to elicit a physical response created by regulating the breath.

Either way, these deceptively simple exercises are at the core of Ninja philosophy and thought. It is believed that when one reaches a certain level of training, the hands automatically form the fingerlocks in times of contemplation or stress. Some schools add chants or mantras, others vigorously rub beads between their hands. Regardless, "the hands are a microcosm of the body," so to stimulate or sedate the flow of energy and blood therein is certain to have an effect, even a mild or moderate one, upon the rest of the system.

By associating specific meanings and symbols to each of these interlocking patterns, the Ninja were able to "program" themselves to withstand any torture or accomplish any feat, thus giving rise to the legends of their superhuman prowess. And while the finger pattern had an effect on the user, it also had an effect on the audience because the knowledge of the connections of the hands are known to everyone, albeit in most cases on a subconscious level.

First, just do the exercise, then learn its many meanings.

Place the tips of your middle fingers together and interlock the other fingers. This represents strength of mind and body. It connects the Yin Yu and Yang Yu Channels of the arm, which flow from the heart. It is also the first step in gaining control of sexual energy.

Place the tips of the index fingers together and wrap the middle fingers around them. This represents direction of energy. It is used to raise consciousness from the lower to the higher levels.

Interlock the middle fingers and the index fingers and extend the third and little fingers with tips touching. This represents harmony with the Universe, and is a therapeutic aid to digestion.

Interlock the middle and ring fingers and extend the index and little fingers with tips touching. This represents healing of self and others, and is beneficial to the kidneys.

Interlock all of the fingers with tips outside. This represents the power of premonition, and symbolizes the heart level.

Interlock all the fingers with tips inside. This represents knowing the thoughts of others, and symbolizes the throat level.

Extend the index finger and thumb with tips touching to form a triangle and spread the other fingers. This represents mastery of time and space, and symbolizes the Jade Pillow at the base of the skull.

Wrap the fingers of the right hand around the left index finger and press against the outside of the fingernail with the thumbnail of the right hand. This represents control of the elements of Nature and symbolizes the pituitary gland.

Wrap the fingers of the right hand around the right thumb and cover the fist with the left open palm. This represents enlightenment and the opening of the Third Eye.

Place the hands in the lap and relax. It feels good to be relaxed, it feels better than before. Every day, in every way, you are getter better and better, so that you may set a good example for all. Pictures of these hand positions are given in *Ninja Mind Control*.

Kuji Kiri is an esoteric part of Ninjitsu, derived from the Buddhist Shugendo sect, which is based on the number 9. In fact, Kuji Kiri means "nine cuts" in Japanese.

All numbers have certain mathematical properties. Any number multiplied by zero becomes zero; any number that is multiplied by one remains the same; nine is the only number that retains its identity regardless of how many times it is multiplied. For example: $2 \times 9 = 18$; $1 + 8 = 9$; $3 \times 9 = 27$, $2 + 7 = 9$; $9 \times 9 = 81$; $12 \times 9 = 108$; and so on ad infinitum. It is for this reason that it was chosen as the basis for Shugendo, to symbolize that the practitioners of that philosophy would retain their own individuality, regardless of the changes they would experience.

This symbolism was not chosen at random. Mathematics is one of the oldest sciences known to man, and reflects the very pattern of the Universe. Zero, the Void, Yin, where there is Nothingness, absorbs all that enters; One is Yang and therefore linear. Two is the number of Yin and Yang; Three symbolizes balance. Four, stability. Five is the number of the Chinese alchemical elements (European systems of alchemy dealt with only four, keeping the fifth element, Wood, a closely guarded secret). Six is the number of life as symbolized by the carbon element of modern physics. Seven, the number of physical planes; Eight the number of change. And nine is the number of completion, before the cycle begins to repeat.

Therefore, there are nine steps in the alchemy of Kuji Kiri:

The All is Mind.
Everything is in vibration.
For every low there is a high.
For every positive there is a negative.
There is an ebb and flow to the tides of the Force.
For every cause there is an effect.
The principle of gender operates on all levels.
What will happen is already written, but one must choose to experience it.
Change is inevitable.

The first seven of these are the Laws of the Hermetic Teachings, representing the principles of mentalism, correspondence, vibration, polarity, rhythm, cause and effect, and gender. The next two are drawn from Taoism. Together these nine laws form the foundation of Ninjitsu, a part of which is Kuji Kiri, the Psionic Martial Art.

Psionics are defined as various powers of the brain that enable one so endowed to perform in ways which resemble magical abilities. All humans possess these latent abilities, but in modern times they are seldom developed for lack of practice and instruction. If psionic abilities are possessed, the number, type, and strength of each must be determined so that one may realize one's full potential and set a good example for all.

These powers and abilities are far beyond those of mortal man, and so cannot be used in a destructive manner because once known, they provide an intuitive understanding of the Universe and one's role in it. Thus selfish motivations, which are considered evil, fall away and are replaced with good intentions, which are of benefit to all mankind.

Now true growth can occur. First, disperse any resistance, then perform the work of rectification. In time, progress will be made. This will be marked by change: movement, disruption, and awakening. One's own nature creates what occurs, and is not at a loss for power to effect it.

Communication is the key. This is the time when the Spirit Helper appears, the guide who will lead the Shadow Self along the Path. This is when one begins to vibrate in harmony with the Universe. It is the journey through the Dark Night of the Soul, when one accepts the will of Heaven and recognizes that as it is above, so below, that the battle of the Mystic Warrior is always with oneself, and that the secret of victory lies in letting go of power. Relinquishing control is the ultimate test of the warrior, more so in light of the fact that the majority of one's practice is aimed at development of that control.

This is the Law of Extremes: that one can be a man of peace and fight like ten tigers. The secret lies in what is willed. Knowing one can prevail gives one confidence that the outcome is assured. Then it can only be that what occurs is what was desired. By knowing oneself and one's place in the cycle of change, the Mystic Warrior exists outside the circle that presses others, and so can affect the affairs of men.

One man, in the right place, at the right time, can change the course of history, if he but choose to do so. This is the role of the Ninja. Just as the Shadow Self is met and incorporated into one's character, so, too, the enemy is at thy mercy and lives or dies at one's discretion. The taking of a life does no one honor, for all life is precious, nor can any be replaced. Therefore it is said that Ninjitsu is a nonviolent martial art.

The "fight or flight" adrenaline response to stress is instinctive in every human being. While most martial arts develop the fight response of meeting force with force, Ninjitsu

teaches how to flee. For this reason, it is known as the Art of
Invisibility.

Ninja are legendary in their ability to endure any hardship,
overcome any obstacle, and prevail against any enemy. Physical, emotional, and spiritual techniques are combined to develop an unbeatable system of self-defense suitable for all ages,
regardless of size, strength, or infirmity.

The Invisible Fist can overcome any attacker simply by
vanishing at will: One cannot hit what one cannot see.

Once removed, attack from ambush. Doing so increases the
likelihood of success times four, and doubles the amount of
damage inflicted. Or vacate the danger area; this is called target
denial. Or, seek sanctuary and call for assistance.

These are the Yin, Yang, and Tao of the Ninja: Avoid rather
than check; check rather than strike; strike rather than kill; and
kill rather than be killed. Never take a hit you don't have to;
never hit until there is an opening; when there is an opening,
hit!

Never strike the first blow, for by so doing, the enemy sets
the pattern for his own defeat. Know the enemy and thyself,
and in one hundred battles you will be victorious. "Know
Thyself" and "Nothing in Excess" were the two phrases written over the entrance to the Oracle of Delphi.

The reason conflict occurs is an excess of one type of
energy—usually Yang, which is aggressive and seeks power.
The logical response is Yin, which is soft and yielding. In this
way the energy is balanced, and one incurs no negative Karma.

If one "wins" a conflict, one makes an enemy. The defeated
will invariably tell the story in such a way that they seem to be
the victor, and will seek to validate this claim at the next
meeting, should there be one. If one "vanishes," the Enemy is
embarrassed, a much less painful injury to his Ego, but one he
will not be eager to repeat. If what you want is to defeat the
enemy, that is an expression of your own power, a stroke for
your Ego.

Thus it is said that the student of Kuji Kiri each day puts
aside more and more, much in the same manner as carving a
stone, or sharpening the edge of a sword, until nothing is left of

the Ego. He does this by becoming one with himself, by developing harmony within himself.

Development of the mind can be achieved only when the body has been disciplined. To accomplish this, the ancients have taught us to imitate the ways of Nature.

There are two kinds of strength, the outer, which fades with age and succumbs to disease, and the inner, which lasts a lifetime and beyond.

Looked for, one cannot be seen; listened for, one cannot be heard; felt for, one cannot be touched. This is the way of the Mystic Warrior, One Who Knows—the Ninja.

Being a Ninja has to do with controlling one's motion in time and space, not with being violent or aggressive. To this end, the ancient masters devised exercises for training the mind and body, as one, to become aware of the myriad shades of existence and other levels of being which exist around us, within us, and through us.

These finger-knitting exercises are derived from the far distant past, beyond the keeping of history; even before rememberers recorded events and tallies on knotted string; back to the beginnings of man himself, when there was only survival and conquest.

As time has passed and the teachings were handed down from master to student, many of the details of these postures have been lost, either through secrecy or forgetfulness, or by simplification to make them understandable to an audience. Yet they remain essentially intact, and indeed, are so powerful and exact that even halfhearted attempts at understanding them lead to revelations of self and the Universe. They cannot be done improperly without soon righting themselves and demonstrating their own proper order for each student. Likewise, by means of their own grading system and slow disclosure of principles, they reveal the exact level at which the student currently resides. Don't think that you can do them with a frivolous attitude, or that you are such a master that you can leap ahead to the advanced techniques. Begin slowly, practice diligently, and then you will learn.

Each of the Nine Levels of Power is known by many names, and by many faces and sounds. With concentration, each level will elicit its own particular visual images. In my travels, I have encountered many who practice some form of meditation. No matter which school they belong to, or to which philosophy they subscribe, all eventually agree that these are the true colors, noises, and sensations which are felt at various stages of development, and which are the signposts to higher levels of consciousness.

In the Tao it is said, "every day less and less is done, until nonaction is achieved; then nothing is left undone," So too with these practices. Eventually, the Ninja may draw upon whatever source of energy is required, for whatever purpose. At this stage, the gestures of the Kuji Kiri flow smoothly from one to another, reminding him of his inner strength and the flow of the Universe. Thus, it was often said that finger-knitting was a way for the Ninja to draw upon mysterious secret powers.

These gestures, or mudras, may also be seen in the body language of ordinary people in everyday life. Finger drumming, for example, is an unconscious, unfocused expression of the same energies, and carries the same meaning. These exercises merely concentrate powers latent in everyone.

Having completed the Kuji Kiri Exercise, either place the hands, still forming the mudra for enlightenment (right fist covered by left hand, symbolizing Yin and Yang, the opposite poles of the Universe in harmony) in the lap and let them relax. Or, place the fists palm up upon the knees with the fingers wrapped around the thumbs to keep energy from "leaking out of the hands" as you meditate. This is a Bandhi, or muscle lock, just as important and powerful as the Sacral, Heart, or Cranial Pump, and may be used to "hold the energy in" or "pump it around" the channels and meridians. The idea is that the tactile stimulation created through the mudras be carried up to the head, then down the body like a flow of warm, relaxing water, to make one sensitive to the experience of inner energy.

Since all life and health depends on respiration, it follows that a student of Ninjitsu must pay particular attention to breathing. The closely related exercises of conscious relaxation and controlled breathing are two of the basic elements in the training process. Indeed, they are of value in ordinary life, quite apart from any specialized training, since they serve to build up and maintain the physical body, and as the body acts upon the mental processes, so a healthy body will act most favorably upon the mind; and since the mind and emotions affect the glandular system of the body, there is a circle of beneficial influence set up which can be of greatest value.

The next step, therefore, is the relaxation exercise. It should be commenced under conditions as free from outer noises as possible. Later, after much practice, the exercise can be carried out even in noisy or otherwise distracting conditions which would have meant failure in the early days. Start by sitting in a comfortable chair, or lying on one's back on a couch or bed.

It is well to point out here that at one point in the exercise a strong muscular spasm or a sudden tensing of the muscles may occur, which very often leads the beginner to think that some type of psychic experience is at hand. Alas, that is not the case. What happens is that, if we are lying flat on our back, we have the weight of the body pressing down upon the whole back of the head, the shoulders, buttocks, and the underside of the thighs and knees, down to the back of the heels. When this position is maintained without movement for some time, the steady pressure upon the nerve endings all over that part of the body creates a sensation of paralysis. We no longer feel the bed beneath us, and for a fraction of a second we seem to be "falling free." Since falling is usually detrimental, our subconscious mind immediately tenses the muscles in a powerful spasm in order to keep the body fixed and safe. I point this out now simply because this experience is so commonly misinterpreted.

Having attained a comfortable position, we are ready to start. It is most important that no article of clothing be tight or in any way uncomfortable. We are going to relax the physical, and do not wish to have messages constantly coming in from various parts of the body calling for relief. Here it may be noted that, for those who prefer the supine position, a pillow should be used to support the neck as well as the back of the head. If not, the head may be forced forward, and breathing restricted.

We now direct our attention to the top of the head, and see if the scalp muscles are tense or relaxed. If the former, and this is usually the case, we deliberately relax them and pass down to the forehead. Here we shall very definitely find the muscles tense, and these should also be relaxed. It will often be found that the muscles of the eyeballs have become involved in this muscular tension, and will also have to be deliberately relaxed. This is not as easy as one might think, especially when one is a beginner. Now we come to the muscles of the face and mouth, and the same procedure is carried out. The muscles of the neck are considered and relaxed, and with them the relaxation of the head is complete.

In case we should be congratulating ourselves on our ability to relax, we can turn our attention back to the top of the head, and in eight out of ten cases we will find that we have unconsciously tensed up the scalp muscles again! So once again we must start to relax consciously. Eventually, we arrive at a point where we have definitely relaxed all the head, face, and throat muscles, and can now move down the trunk to the arms, legs, and finally, the feet. It has been said that the effect of this exercise is that one "rests on the waters of peace."

Invoking Your Spirit Helpers

"The way is known to all, but not all know it."

When you obtained this book it was because you were in search of occult power. You wanted to know the secrets that would make you invulnerable. It has been said that no one may find this without personal instruction by one skilled in the dark arts. And that is so.

So how may we contact these secret sensei? The answer is simple: We must follow their example. True knowledge endures without regard for the sands of time, and the immutable laws of the Universe carry each of us to our fate whether we take notice or not. There are many paths to the Universal Mind, the Cosmic Consciousness. One may follow the Eightfold Path and grow, or embrace the way of the spiritual devotee; all lead to the dwelling place of Vishnu, who knows all, sees all, and tells all. At this level of mind, anything is possible.

Then, if we seek to become one with nature and experience communion with this all-wise consciousness, and concede that we conceive it as being outside ourselves, we feel loneliness, which causes us to seek the counsel of others. Most people are motivated by self-interest, so there are those who would take advantage of this motivation. Finally we are left completely abandoned. This is the Dark Night of the Soul, when one decides between life and death and finds the Inner Strength, with or without "help." Every living being passes through this test of self-doubt.

Many cultures have secret ceremonies whereby one may find or summon this spiritual advisor, and of course everyone has a different concept of the appearance or mode of communication of this being. For most, invoking this spiritual guidance is automatic and unconscious. One may remember a beloved relative, or a combination of several people who have had a powerful or guiding influence. Even a figure from history may appear to counsel you. For some it may be that little voice of conscience that keeps us out of trouble most of the time. So long as we are aware of the benevolent and guiding nature of these familiars, we may be assured of their assistance and support on our behalf. The more frequently they are consulted, the more influence they have and the greater the ease with which they are contacted.

History and experience has shown that whatever form these imaginary friends may take, they have certain common characteristics. Since they represent authority figures, all are firm and honest in their advice and directions. Since they are the idealized creation of a teacher or sage, they are never upset or angry, and their explanations or flashes of insight fully answer and explain any question. This invariably has a calming effect on the student and helps to calm any fears or anxiety. Lastly, since they are friends, they possess a sense of irony and humor, which enables us to see ourselves as others see us and realize that most of our problems are self-induced and really of little consequence in the scheme of the Universe. This leads to humility.

There are hundreds of meditation techniques. Each relies on artificially altering the chemical state of the blood either by deep breathing (hyperventilating) or holding the breath (hypoventilating). Each must be practiced carefully, lest the increased oxygen in the bloodstream makes one conscious of the heartbeat. In many cases, this leads to anxiety, but is easily calmed by simply holding the breath for a moment. Charlatans may insist that this phenomenon is the result of some manipulation of their own when, in fact, it is a simple physiological effect.

Therefore, we present only the most rudimentary method, which, with patient practice over a long period, will lead the curious to discover any others that may be required. Rudyard Kipling wrote, "there is a certain calming influence that one may experience by the mere assumption of a comfortable position and the slow repetition of one's name." Such a practice also develops an awareness of Self, and an understanding of the same. Therefore, to request of the Hidden Masters an ally who may act as sentry, scout, or spy, who is in contact with the Universal Mind of all mankind and has access to all things and knowledge, hidden or revealed, one must make some preparation.

In the 1920s and 1930s—and up to the present day—the United States was inundated by spiritualists and mediums who claimed miraculous curative powers far beyond those of mortal men. They possessed, so the story goes, a "spirit guide" from beyond the pale of this human plane, with whom they communicated while in a deep, trancelike state. During these manifestations, the "spirit guide" was able to speak through the medium's voice, although the voices of each were distinctly dissimilar. We shall not attempt so profound a materialization at this juncture, but it should be noted that these were merely persons who acknowledged an imaginary friend publicly.

While the degree of detail is attributed to the ally contributes greatly to its realism and subsequent effectiveness, one should not become so enamored of the fantasy relationship that it takes precedence over reality. But, as a child, "making believe," "pretending," suspending for a few moments the press of everyday life allows a certain surcease from the crush of responsibility. And that is called reducing stress.

You may decide beforehand what type of familiar you desire, and prepare with sketches or descriptive poetry, all of which enhance the experience. But in the end, it is the subconscious which determines the form you will perceive. If the form you decided on is similar to the one your subconscious delivers to your conscious mind, then you already possess significant personal insight and self-knowledge. If not, then the High Self will most often be the counterpoint of the child facet of one's personality, thereby balancing Yin and Yang in the adult self which must function in the real world.

Lie down in a comfortable position so that all parts of the body are equally supported. Close your eyes. Become aware of the sounds around you, not distracted by them, just aware. Inhale deeply and fully without strain as you mentally count, one, two, three, four. At first the speed of the count will reflect your conscious state of mind. Later, it will synchronize with your heartbeat. Finally, it will regulate the heartbeat. Hold the inhalation for one, two. Relax and let the air flow easily out of the lungs as you count, one, two, three, four. Hold the exhalation for one, two. Repeat this three times.

When retaining the inhaled breath, do not constrict the muscles of the throat, as this will damage the blood vessels in the neck and face. On the exhalation, hold the air out with the Tan T'ien, or Hara.

Think of the most pleasant experience you have ever had. Then, take three deep breaths and as you exhale each time, count backwards from three to one. This is a deepening exercise which enables one to develop a more contemplative state. It also focuses the attention on breathing, which helps to elicit what some Boston researchers have described as the "relaxation response" present in all humans. Feel that relaxation in the body. Do not let any sounds you may hear distract you from this contemplation. If left to chance, most people will drift easily from this state into a light sleep.

The Ninja have a saying, "All men have three names, the one they are called, the one they are known by, and the one they share with no one else." So, too, it is with the Spirit Helper. Having decided to make this contact, we may either do so leisurely, by waiting for it to appear to us and then be named, or we may seek to contact a specific entity, in which event the procedure now requires that you speak the name you have chosen. Repeat it three times, softly.

This will be your own personal mantra. Do not tell it to anyone else, since to do so invites comparison or criticism from those less imaginative. Communication with this alter ego may take many forms: verbal, visual, kinesthetic, or even telepathy, since that is a dialogue of two minds.

Look for me in the sky of a summer day. . . . Listen for the sound of my footsteps on the path. . . . Lift the rock and I am there.

—Cheyenne Indian chant

"I have no friend; I make my mind my friend." These words are taught in Zen meditation and are part of the Japanese creed of the samurai. The Ninja carry this one step further. HsiMen-Jitsu, the Chinese art of psychology (literally the "Way of the Mind Gate"), teaches that there are three facets of every personality. Dr. Eric Berne called them child, adult, and internalized parent; the ancients referred to them as Heaven, Earth and Man (Shen, Ch'i, and Ching). The Hidden Masters are the "high self", the Jonin, the "upper man", the internalized mores and behaviors we have learned from authority figures. This serves three functions: first, it enables one to act as an actual parent, thus promoting survival of the race; second, it makes many responses automatic in accordance with the principle of cause and effect; and third, it acts as a counsel and guide when we are lost, a friend when we are alone, and a teacher of the secret knowledge. Everyone has such an ally who can be trusted completely and consulted on any question.

Invocation These are the chants and mantras used either aloud when applied hypnotically, or through memory when administered internally, that lead the seeker to the source of his internal power, which he may then bring into the "real" world to work his will.

They should be spoken or mentally recited in the middle of the Longevity Exercise, at the point after the Six Healing Breaths or Sounds has been completed and at the end of the Kuji Kiri exercise, which signals the body that the energy will "run up the spine" and opens the "gates" in a kinesthetic or mnemonic manner. Now, we are going to imagine it. Once the first channel, the Tu Mo, is opened, it is a simple matter to visualize the Jen Mo and other channels and direct the Qi along them mentally. In Hindu Yoga, they open the Jen Mo, on the front of the body first, but the Chinese go up the Heavenly Pillar.

There are, of course, a great many other ways of regulating the respiration, any of which may be inserted at this point to elicit the desired effect from the meditative state. But in the final analysis, sitting quietly, taking long, slow, deep breaths, thinking of nothing, is where all your answers lie.

The questions that have plagued mankind for all his time on the planet, which have not really changed throughout the generations, are transcendent. Any attempt to describe them or label them falls well short of satisfactory. Therefore, the only proof of their validity lies in "experiencing" the moment between life and death, when all things are made clear.

These signs and guideposts merely point the way to such a "transcendental experience," which occurs as a result of the inner quest for self-knowledge.

The first part of the Longevity Set prepares you for this moment of relaxation, the second part, described in another section, is the "awakening from the Dream-Time"—movements that return you to the physical reality of this moment.

Imagine you are outside.
Beneath the night sky.

"The best time is the Hour of Tzu, between 11 P.M. and 1
   A.M. when the energy of the Earth is rising toward the
   night sky.
Select a place where you can sit or lie quietly, unobserved.
Make yourself comfortable there.
Take a deep breath and look up at the stars.
Behold the only thing greater than yourself.
The Universe.
Compared to this, we are as insignificant as a grain of
   sand beside a boundless ocean.
But a grain of sand, nonetheless.
Without which nothing exists and through which all
   things are possible.
And it is by will alone that I set my mind in motion, to
   shake the web of Heaven, to touch the fabric of
   Universe, to make my dream reality.
I have no parents, I make Heaven and the Earth my
   parents.
I have no home, I make the center of the Universe my
   home.
I have no divine power, I make honesty my power.
I have no means, I make docility my means.
I have no magic, I make personality my magic.
I have no body, I make stoicism my body.
I have no eyes, I make the flash of lightning my eyes.
I have no ears, I make sensibility my ears.
I have no limbs, I make promptitude my limbs.
I have no laws, I make self-protection my laws.
I have no strategy, I make the right to kill and restore to
   life my strategy.
I have no designs, I make seizing opportunity by the
   forelock my design.
I have no principles, I make adaptability to all
   circumstances my principles.
I have no tactics, I make emptiness and fullness my
   tactics.
I have no talent, I make ready wit my talent.

I have no friends, I make my mind my friend.

I have no enemy, I make incautiousness my enemy.

I have no armor, I make benevolence my armor.

I have no castle, I make immovable mind my castle.

I have no sword, I make no-mind my sword.

I have no miracles, I make righteous laws my miracle.

I have neither life nor death, I make every breath my life and death.

I have no heroes, I make every act my last act on Earth, I am the hero of my own life.

I think, therefore, I am.

And I am that I may continue to be and have always been.

I am only one.

But because I am one, I shall do all that I can to strive for the perfection of character, foster the spirit of effort, honor the principles of etiquette, defend the paths of truth, and guard against impetuous courage.

I am the Chosen, because I choose to be.

A brother of the arcane order, a friend to all the world.

I have no name, no art.

I come from no school, I practice no acknowledged style or system.

I am my own man.

I train myself, so that I may be my own master.

So that I may be of service to others.

I am nothing, my cup is empty.

Fill me with your teaching, Sensei, so that I too may set a good example for all...and become a man of knowledge.

It all begins with the breath.

Audiotapes of this and other meditative chants and mantras are available. Please write to Dojo Press, P.O. Box 209, Lake Alfred, FL 33850 for further information.

The Eight Psychic Channels

This incantation or chant should be spoken or recited mentally at the conclusion of the Samurai Creed, the previous deepening exercise.

The chant is the means whereby you will become "present" in your Dream-Time, or auto-hypnotic state, induced by the whole sequence of preceding exercises. The Body of Light mentioned in the chant represents the "astral Self," which can travel in the realm of imagination and memory, and make the journey to the "secret place" to meet the "hidden teacher."

The Body of Light created by the Eight Psychic Channels Exercise is a symbol of the physical body. It will be imagined to be as detailed as necessary for the student to experience "lucid dreaming," a feeling of "being present" in the dream rather than being merely an observer, which is the way most dreams are played out.

Another method for accomplishing this is the Yaqui Indian method of telling yourself when you go to bed that you will dream and in that dream you will see your hands. Since these are familiar objects, and you have often watched them perform a variety of tasks, it is easy to link memory and imagination by this simple trick. Observe that later on, in the guided meditation monologue, there is a reference to looking at the hands, and that from the outset, we have made a point of describing the hands, rubbing the hands, knitting the fingers together, and so on to enhance this mental image for this stage of development.

Some Kung Fu Schools use only the channels that flow from the solar plexus and feed the arm (the Yin and Yang Yu Channels) to charge the hands and develop the Iron Palm, which is capable of killing an opponent by disrupting his Qi with an "internal strike" (like the rupturing of the spleen), without leaving a mark on the outside of the body. The training method is to stand in water up to your waist with a $12 \times 12 \times$ 1-inch board floating in front of you. Then hang a bundle of incense sticks from a limb growing out over the pond or pool, at solar plexus level. Hold your hand palm down underneath the sticks of incense until you can feel the heat on the back of your hand, then slap down on the board in an attempt to break it. (Tamieshiwara is a common breaking test in many Karate schools, using white or yellow pine boards of the appropriate dimensions between two upright supports. This is much easier than trying to break a board floating on a pond without support at either end, and is the same position in which to place the board when taking the Iron Body test. It makes the weakest, most unsupported part the target, or point of impact.) Just keep trying this until you break the board, then get another one. This practice technique is intended to simulate what the Iron Palm Master feels when he channels his Qi to his fist, so it essentially tells the student what to look for, or feel for, when meditating. At first you think it can't be done. Then you get bored and your palm hurts, you stop thinking about it—and then you discover you have broken the thing.

There are entire schools of Kung Fu based on this principle. But the Ninja know that it is only one small part of the Iron Body, which is only a small part of learning to be invisible.

The root of the Eight Psychic Channels is the Gate of Mortality at the base of the genital organs. This is linked with the Tu Mo at the base of the spine, and is joined in the brain by the Jen Mo.

From the center of the brain (pineal gland) it descends through the center of the head to the palate, or Heavenly Pool. This is connected to the jaw, and the system is used in meditation and breathing to allow the Qi to be collected, refined, and escape.

Under the palate, the channel goes down the throat, through the pulmonary artery to the hepatic artery, past and under the diaphragm, behind the solar plexus, below the navel, and back to the root of the genitals.

Thus, as in the meridians of acupuncture, the system forms a complete circuit, beginning and ending at the genitals.

—from Da Liu

(Refer to the Map of the Body to trace this circuit.) Now I want you to begin to practice the method of the Eight Mystic Trigrams...

So that you may create the Body of Light...
And be present in the Dream World...
And journey to your Secret Place.
Breathe in...
Filling the lungs from bottom to top...
And letting the Qi rise up the back...
In four heartbeats.
Hold the breath for two beats.
Breathe out in four heartbeats...
Letting the Qi flow down the front of the body to the
    Needle at the Bottom of the Sea.
Hold the No-Breath for two heartbeats.
Breathe in, drawing the Qi upward...
Around the waist...
Up the back to the shoulders.
Pause.
Breathe out, letting the Qi flow down the backs of the
    arms...
To the tips of the middle fingers.
Pause.
Breathe in, drawing the Qi up the inside of the arms...
From the centers of the palms...
To the shoulders, at the Wind Point.
Pause.
Breathe out, letting the Qi flow down the front of the body
    to the Needle at the Bottom of the Sea.
Pause.
Breathe in, lifting the energy up the center of the body to
    the solar plexus level.
Pause.
Breathe out, letting the Qi flow down from the heart,
    down the outside of the legs...
To the arch of the foot.
Pause.

Breathe in, drawing the Qi up the inside of the legs...
To the Tan T'ien.
Pause.
Breathe out.
Relax, and let the Qi settle and circulate in the Hara.
These are the Eight Psychic Channels that compose the
    Inner Body of Light.
Only the first two correspond and have related points on
    the twelve meridians that compose the physical body.
You are now completely relaxed.
At a deeper, healthier level of mind.
Feeling better than before.

Chart of the Eight Psychic Channels

Channel of Control (Tu Mo)   This begins at the coccyx,
continues up the spine and over the skull, ending at the upper
gum. Recall that Qi is collected from the breath in the Heavenly
Pool of the palate. Qi from the Hara is raised up the Tu Mo by
means of the Sacral Pump. This is analogous to the Kundalini
energy extracted by Pranayama exercises in Hatha Yoga, and
represents the parasympathetic nervous system.

Channel of Function (Jen Mo)   Beginning at the base of the
genitals (the Needle at the Bottom of the Sea Point or Perineum
one), it travels up the front of the body, ending on the face
below the chin. It is joined with the Tu Mo in the Heavenly Pool
by touching the tip of the tongue to the roof of the mouth. It
represents the sympathetic nervous system. When these two
are united the student gains conscious mental control of many
autonomic responses and functions.

Belt Channel (Tai Mo)   This channel connects the Tu Mo and
Jen Mo at the level of the waist, encircling the belly at the navel.
Its function is to act as a reservoir of Qi for the meridians
concerned with proper digestion and elimination.

Thrusting Channel (Ch'ueng Mo)   This channel begins at the
Perineum point and travels up the center of the body to the
solar plexus level. It is directly related to the Heart Pump.

CHART OF THE EIGHT PSYCHIC CHANNELS

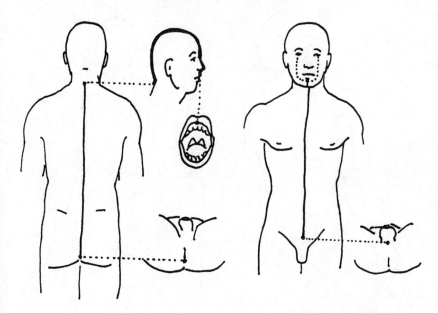

Channel of Control   **Channel of Function**

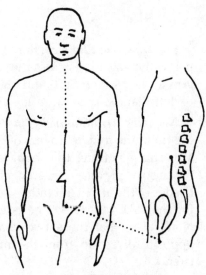

Belt Channel   **Thrusting Channel**

CHART OF THE EIGHT PSYCHIC CHANNELS

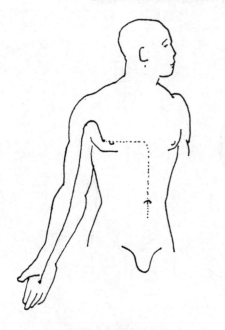
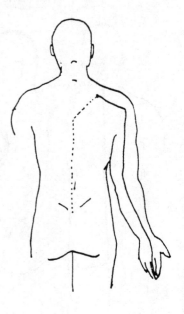

Positive Arm Channel   **Negative Arm Channel**

Positive Arm Channel (Yang Yu Mo)   This channel rises from below the navel, up across the chest and down the inside of the arm to the Dragon (left) and Tiger (right) cavities in the centers of both hands, then on to the tips of the middle fingers.

Negative Arm Channel (Yin Yu Mo)   This channel rises from the tip of the middle fingers of each hand, up the outside of the arm and penetrates the shoulder through the armpit and back to the solar plexus. The actual channel is taught to be inside the tissues of the arm itself rather than near the outside surface, but for the sake of clarity, one is considered inside and one out. Note, also, that these two channels of the arm flow in the opposite direction from the meridians, which are displayed later.

CHART OF THE EIGHT PSYCHIC CHANNELS

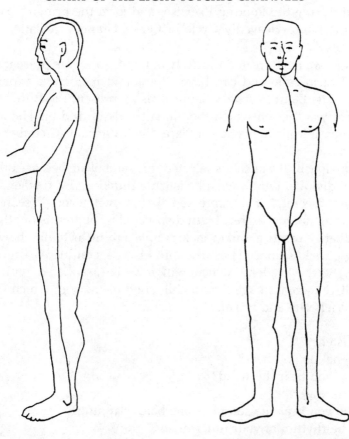

Positive Leg Channel   **Negative Leg Channel**

Positive Leg Channel (Yang Chiao Mo) This channel rises from the heel, turns along the the outer sides of the legs and ankles, up the sides of the body, around the head, and down to the ear.

Negative Leg Channel (Yin Chiao Mo) This channel rises from the instep up the inner leg, past the groin, through the center of the body to the site of the Third Eye, between and slightly above the eyebrows. It is these two channels which are used during the Rooting Exercise, and form the primary path for the Large Heavenly Cycle of Qi, or Grand Circulation of Energy.

Now we have created the Body of Light, so we are present in the Dream-Time and can have a profound meditative experience. The Eight Psychic Channels also represent the Path, the "silent way," upon which the Ninja treads to find his Hidden Teacher. It leads to his Secret Place, the Mysterious Chamber of the mind.

Obviously, the ancients selected this symbolism because only the individual knows what he is truly thinking. Even when he tells a "secret," it is expressed in his own terms—"secret" meaning not just a great truth discovered through this or other meditative practice, but even so simple a thing as telling how a magic trick is done. Thus, the mind is a "secret place" known only to the student, which will now be associated with a positive mental image, i.e., a childhood memory in which the child felt safe and warm.

Listen.
What do you hear?
Do you hear the wind?
The water?
Do you hear the sound of one hand clapping?
The rhythm of your inner drum?
It is the beating of your heart that provides comfort and
    reassurance, and quiet relaxation.
Feel your lungs filling with air...
Your heart pumping...
Arteries surging with life...
The energy of your being flowing about you.
You are one with the Universe...
Full and complete...
And it is good to be alive.
Now I want you to go to your secret place...
A place known only to you...
Where you are always safe and welcome...

Where everything you need to solve any problem or
   answer any question lies waiting...
A place where all your dreams come true.
Do it now.
Be there now.
Move forward through the darkness, like a blind man, lost
   in some vast forgotten hall, with no floor, no echo of
   footsteps, nothing to bar one's path.
Only the Self...
The Mind... the "'I' that I am" and shall always be, and
   have always been.
The captain of my Fate... The Master of my Soul.
Reach out with your mind.
Fill the Void with the powers of memory and imagination,
   create the dream that is your Universe.
Gaze into the darkness and say to yourself...
Let there be light...
And lo, there is light.
This is your Secret Place, a place known only to you.
Where you are always safe and welcome, and where all
   your wishes come true.

Poetry is an excellent way to induce a deeper level of mind. It
is rhythmic, alliterative, has cadence, and in most cases
rhymes, making it easier to remember. It might be considered
an advanced form of chanting, in that it elicits a physiological
response with a verbal cue. If it is recited aloud or in a
whisper, it regulates the breath. If it is recited mentally, it may
elicit an emotion, a (tactile) sensation, or a visual image. Be
alert for poetry that you find imaginatively suggestive or
appealingly rhythmic to use as a vehicle for meditation.

Be there now.
Lungs filling with air...
Heart pumping...
Arteries surging...

Energy flowing.
To breathe again.
To be again.
To see, hear, and touch again.
You are a child of the Universe...
And you are not alone.
We knew you would come.
We have been waiting to welcome you.
Your name is "I-trey-u."
(Reversed or mirrored phonetically, "You are it.")
Your Way lies across the water.
You are the Chosen...
The Golden Child.
The Elected One, among the many.
Now it's time for you to meet your Spirit Helper...
The Dream Weaver of your Soul...
Who is always with you...
And guides your steps by confirming the signs and
    portents along the Way.
The Spirit Helper may manifest itself in many ways...
But it will always be the first living creature you see in
    your Secret Place.
Some see an animal.
Some see the face of a loved one who has passed on
    before, a Guardian Angel.
Some see themselves.
This is the purpose of the Dream Weaver...
To lead you to the Sacred Pool of the Subconscious...
The Magic Mirror of the Soul...
That you may know your Self...
That you may understand others...
That you may set a good example for all.
From your Spirit Helper, your Shadow Self, you will learn
    the laws of the Universe...
The rules of the Game of Self-Knowledge...
The keys to understanding.
The great principle of the Universe is change.

In the Void, the Yin, there is nothing.

Then the Yang stirs, and there is movement.

Then these two strive for balance...And are manifest as the Universe.

One cannot explain such things.

One must know them on an intuitive level.

They must be experienced.

Speak to your Spirit Helper.

Say his name

It is a secret name...

Known only to you.

Say it now...

Say it now...

Say it now...

And each time you say it, you will know that he is with you.

O Sensei, great teacher, thank you for another day.

Let me strive to make my life better and better in every way,

So that I may set a good example for all.

Let me take what comes with a smile...

And bear malice toward no man.

O Sensei, Great Teacher, source of all light and power in the world...

Shine also into my heart, so that I too may accomplish the Great Work.

For I live to serve your higher purpose, in this strand of Time.

Thank you for showing me the Path and for helping me to walk it.

Make me healthy, wealthy, and wise, that I may be of service to my fellow man.

And let the light of your teaching shine through me...

That all may see, and I may set a good example for all...

For I ask in the name of Grand-Father, the Great Spirit.

Amen.

The Self forms the "adult" component of the personality, the higher self, or internalized parent and authority figure, which keeps balance between the "child," or lower self, represented by the three lower chakras of Hindu cosmology and which are also the psychological components of the survival level of consciousness—food, water, shelter, and reproduction—all of which require immediate gratification. The higher self's function is to provide inhibitions and injunctions to prevent the child self from "acting out" with constant demands which must be immediately gratified. The purpose of the meditation is to introduce these three components to each other by letting the child play with its imagination; by acknowledging the adult self with physical sensations such as breathing and heartbeat, which are generally overlooked or ignored as autonomic; and by approaching the higher self with an air of reverence and respect, since it is this figure which must be "answered to," either out of self-pride or a guilty conscience. From this source flow all punishments and rewards. Therefore, an understanding of this figure is essential to properly integrating the personality, which can only be done on an individual level. Thus, it cannot be explained, but it can be experienced. Poetry and repetition are used to progressively deepen the level of relaxation until this is possible. The higher self represents memory.

Behold, the Dream Weaver comes.
I seek to know, so I may be of service.
Speak friend and enter.

This is the key that opens the Door to Knowledge in the
    Halls of Learning.
For only one who is pure of heart may enter there.
One must be taken to these doorways by a Guide.
One who has passed this way before, and shares what has
    been found. Each seeker is one of his ten. (Remember
    the "oath.")
There are many paths.
A Seeker may choose freely from among them.

For they all lead to the same treasure.

Each is merely a step in the pattern of the Universe. And
   they may run parallel to or intersect with other paths
   and other Seekers. Doors and gates may be passed or
   entered. But, if they are on the way the Seeker has
   chosen, what lies behind them will be made known.

What will happen in the life of a Seeker is already written;
   but, one must choose to be there. Thus, free will and
   predestination exist simultaneously.

By encountering or selecting Guides, one begins to vibrate
   in harmony with the fabric of the Universe, and,
   likewise, to set it vibrating.

Life is a river.

One may fight upstream,

One may swim with the current,

Or, one may be carried along with the ebb and flow of the
   Universe.

This is one Path.

For a long time, you have been traveling...

Taking a journey that was indicated in the palm of your
   hand.

You have searched for a Teacher...

To walk the line in your palm with you...

For a moment...

A guide, to point out the landmarks and signposts along
   the way.

And now, you have found him.

I am your Hidden Teacher...

Looked for cannot be seen, listened for cannot be heard,
   felt for cannot be touched.

I come from the no-place, and I go to the nowhere.

I have no magic power.

Anyone can do the things I do...

If they but know how.

I cannot describe to you the indescribable...

But I can teach you several, by no means inconsiderable,
   arts...

Invisibility, flying without wings, knowing the thoughts of

others, invulnerability to sword or serpent's fang...
That sort of thing.
I am that I am, friend to all the world.
I place upon you my mark against evil so that no harm
    will befall you as we step upon the moonlit path...
And begin the Inner Journey.
You have endured many trials and tests to have come this
    far, alone...
And very frightening, indeed, they must have been.
But what you are about to learn now may be even more
    alarming.
All that is required is a momentary suspension of your
    disbelief...
And faith that we shall never injure or embarrass you in
    any way.
You can stop now...
Without looking in the book.
One should not step lightly onto this path...
For it will change your life forever.
You will never be the same again...
The Seekers fight their way here, year after year, eager to
    pay a terrible price, to suffer any pain, indignity, or
    sacrifice...
To enter the halls of learning and discover Knowledge...
To look in the Book of Secrets.
And, when they fling it open, in blazing expectation of
    finding the answers to all life's questions...
What do they find?
Themselves.
There is no enlightenment.
There is nothing to take back, no great secret.
Only your Self.
And the Great Game.
You can ignore the Game, or keep it a secret, or you can
    choose to play...
And that is what you have done.
You are the Chosen.

What you see here, what you say here, when you leave
here, it will stay here...

Waiting for your return.

And each time you use the keys of patience, practice, and
perseverance to come here...

You will learn more, and faster, and remember the lessons
you receive...

So that you may bring them into your waking life,

And become better than before. So that good deeds will
spread out like the ripples on a pond and make the
world a better place. In this way one becomes a Ninja, a
man of knowledge, a good example for all.

So it is written, so it is done.

This wisdom is not dispensed lightly...

Nor to the unworthy.

It is forbidden to use this knowledge for personal gain.

Only the pure of heart may pass the between the pillars of
Good and Evil.

The Way lies before you.

Say to yourself, "friend"...

And step upon the Golden Path, listen to the Silent
Flute...

The Dream Weaver's whisper in your ear.

The mood of the warrior is waiting...

Waiting, some say, for his enemy to appear.

But the true Ninja (mystic-warrior) knows that there are
no enemies but himself...

And that all those who appear as enemies are merely pale
reflections of his own dark self.

They come to him to test themselves...

And in losing, they gain their victory.

For then they stand on the threshold of Truth...

And that gift, which is what they really want from you...

They will have it then.

Thus, the true warrior waits not for the enemies of Anger,
Greed, Lust, Ego, Envy, Irreligiosity, Violence,
Ignorance, Bad Company, Jealousy, and Deceit, nor

clouds his mind with the delusion that the reality of this
moment is the reality of all moments.
The true warrior purifies his Spirit...
Which leads to Mercy...
Which leads to Charity...
Which leads to Right Conduct...
Which leads to Selfless Service...
Which leads to Apt Religion...
Which leads to Right Knowledge...
Which leads to Spiritual Devotion.
This is the Eightfold Path of the Mystic Trigram.
It confers upon the warrior the armor of Righteousness.
It is his fortress and defense, against all enemies, visible
and invisible.
In this, and every magical work...
The wise man walks with his head bowed...
Humble as the dust.
This is his Cloak of Invisibility...
A riddle, wrapped in a question, surrounded by a mystery.
A man of peace who can fight like ten tigers.
A warrior...
Waiting for his Will...
To set a good example for all.
Though his light is hidden...
He shines nonetheless...
And now, you are one of us.
Here, then, is your syllabus of study.
Seeking the Mysterious Portal, you must first have an
understanding of Yin and Yang...
Then acknowledge the Five Elements, so that you may
render yourself invisible and enter the Temple of
Heaven.
Next, the Eight Mystic Trigrams, so that you may fly to the
Mysterious Chamber.
Wrestle with the forces that guard the Golden Elixir...
Defeat them, and return to Earth an Immortal.
Such things are not mastered in a single day.

The keys to success are patience, practice, and
   perseverance.
You must be strong, you must know, you must dare, and
   you must remain silent.
One of your skill and determination has but to follow this
   course of instruction to be certain of success.
Take a chance.
Dare to be great.
Live your life as an exclamation instead of an explanation.
Be the captain of your fate, the master of your Soul.
There is no one else.
If not you, who?
If not now, when?
We are the Gray Ones, the invisible tribe...
Keepers of the ancient wisdom, guardians of the sacred
   trust, warriors of the vision quest...
Who perform the glittering magical work of the mystic
   Laughing Light.
We welcome you to our brotherhood as a man of peace
   who can fight like ten tigers.
You have come to us to test yourself...
And, by yielding, you have gained your victory.
For now, you stand on the threshold of Truth...
And that gift, which is what you really wanted from us...
You have it now.

THE TWELVE MERIDIANS

The purpose of the following exercise is to spread the internal
awareness, developed and focused inside the body through
the previous techniques, back into the external body, i.e., the
one in "reality." This is part of the "awakening" from the
Dream-Time. We accomplish this by directing the Qi along the
pathways, or meridians, identified by the ancient art of
acupuncture.

Now I want you to practice the Method of the Twelve
Meridians, which controls the circulation of energy among the

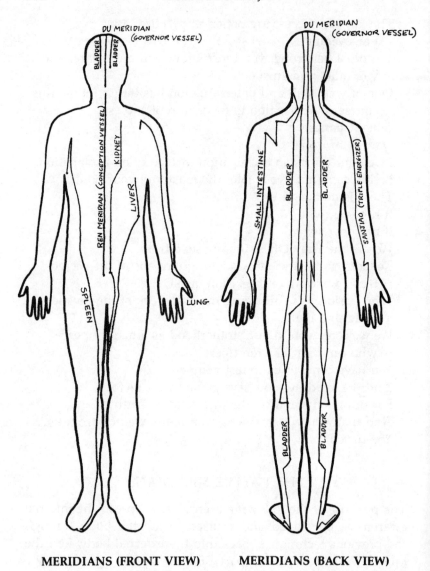

MERIDIANS (FRONT VIEW)   MERIDIANS (BACK VIEW)

Five Elements that compose the Physical Self. They must be learned in precisely this sequence, as this is the true circulation of Qi. In accordance with the Law of Midday and Midnight, it begins at the Hour of Tzu, with the breath.

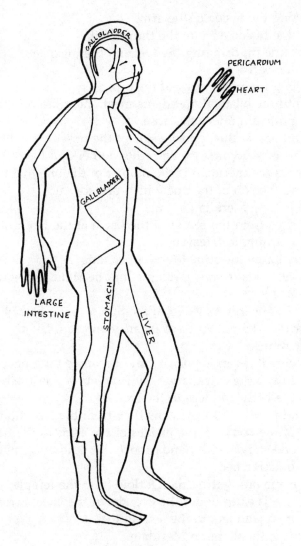

MERIDIANS (SIDE VIEW)

Take a deep breath, filling the lungs with fresh, pure,
    wholesome air.
Breathe out, letting the Qi flow from the Wind Point,
On the front of the shoulder,

Along the inside of the arm,
To the inside edge of the thumbnail.
Breathe in, bringing the Qi from the inside edge of the
    index finger,
Along the upper back of the arm,
Until the bilateral meridians meet and cross on the
    philtrum under the nose,
And end at the opposite side of the nose.
This is in accordance with the Mother-Son Law,
That each meridian is the mother of the one that follows it,
And the son of the one which precedes it.
The Lung Meridian is Yin.
It rises from the center of the Earth at the Hour of Tzu,
    reaching for Heaven.
The Large Intestine Meridian is Yang.
It descends from Heaven during the Hour of Chou, (1 to 3
    A.M.),
Just as energy flows from the Sun to the center of the
Earth, where it reverses polarity and returns to
Heaven as Yin,
Where it reverses polarity and becomes Yang once more.
All the Yang meridians flow from above, on the back of
    the body and legs to the feet.
And all the Yin meridians flow from the feet, up the front
    of the body, up the insides of the arms to the fingertips,
If one stands with hands above the head and fingers
    outstretched.
Breathe out, letting the Qi flow from the temple,
To the jaw, up under the eye, down the cheek, front of the
    body and leg, to the second toe.
This is the Stomach Meridian.
It is a Yang meridian and represents the Earth element.
Breathe in, letting the Qi rise from the foot, up the inside
    of the leg and torso to the top of the breast, then down
    the side to the ribs under the arm.
This is the Spleen Meridian.
It is Yin, and represents the Earth element.
The Hour of the Stomach is Yin (3 to 5 A.M).

Of the Spleen is Mao (5 to 7 A.M.)

Breathe out, letting the Qi flow along the inside of the arm to the tip of the little finger.

This is the Heart Meridian,

Predominant at the Hour of Chen (7 to 9 A.M.).

It is a Yin meridian, representing the Fire element.

Breathe in, letting the Qi flow from the outside edge of the little fingernail, along the back of the arm, across the shoulder blades, up the neck to the base of the ear, forward to the cheek, and back to the top of the ear.This is the Small Intestine Meridian,

Predominant at the Hour of Ssu (9 to 11 A.M.).

It is a Yang meridian, representing Fire.

Breathe out, letting the Qi flow from the inside corner of the eye, over the top of the head, down the back, the back of the legs, under the ankle, to the outside edge of the little toenail.

This is the Bladder Meridian.

It is strongest during the Hour of Wu (11 A.M. to 1 P.M.).

It is a Yin meridian, symbolizing the Water element.

Breathe in, bringing the Qi up from the Bubbling Well Point on the sole of the foot, along the inside of the leg to the groin, up the front of the torso to the clavicle (collarbone).

This is the Kidney Meridian,

Strongest at the hour of Wei (1 to 3 P.M.).

It is a Yang meridian, symbolizing Water.

Breathe out, letting the Qi flow along the inside of the arm from the nipples to the tips of the middle fingers.

This is the Heart Governor (Pericardium/Circulation-Sex) Meridian.

It is full of energy between the hours of 3 and 5 P.M., the Hour of Shen.

A Yin meridian, its element is Fire.

Breathe in, bringing the Qi along the outside of the arm from the ring finger to the bottom of the ear, around the back of the ear to the top, then forward to the outside edge of the eye.

This is the Triple Warmer Meridian.

Its energy is full between 5 and 7 P.M., the Hour of Yu.

A Yang meridian, its element is also Fire.

Breathe out, letting the Qi flow from the outside corner of the eye to the bottom of the ear, to the outside edge of the eyebrow, up, around the temple, to the top of the ear, the base of the skull, up to the hairline above the eyebrow, down the back of the skull and neck to the shoulder, down the side of the body and front of the leg, across the top of the foot to the third toe.

This is the Gall Bladder Meridian.

It is full of energy at the hour of Hsu (7 to 9 P.M.).

It is a Yang meridian, representing the Wood element.

Breathe in, bringing the Qi up from the big toe, along the inside of the leg to the hips, then up to the tip of the lowest floating rib on the torso..

This is the Liver Meridian,

It is fullest of energy during the Hour of Hai (9 to 11 P.M.).

It is a Yin meridian, representing the Wood element.

These are the twelve meridians of acupuncture.

But the points need not be pierced, nor the Qi stirred,

So long as the Qi flows smoothly and evenly from one to the next in the proper sequence.

This exercise cures and prevents many illnesses.

And is used to restore mental concentration to the physical Self,

Returning, by these means, from the Dream-Time,

To the realm of Reality.

Breathe out.

Relax and let the Qi settle to the Hara.

Breathe in and bring the energy up the back from the coccyx to the top of the head, to the upper lip.

This is the Governing Vessel Meridian.

It corresponds with the the the Tu Mo, or first psychic channel and represents the autonomic nervous system.

Breathe out, and let the Qi flow down the front of the body to the Hara.

Breathe in, and bring the Qi up the front of the body from
the Needle at the Bottom of the Sea to the lower lip.
This is the Conception Vessel Meridian.
It corresponds to the Jen Mo, or second psychic channel
and represents the voluntary nervous system.
These two extraordinary meridians are neither Yin nor
Yang.
Qi circulates in them constantly.
This is the Small Heavenly Cycle of Qi...
From whence we began the Inner Journey...
From whence we now return...
And awaken the physical Self.
Breathe out, and let all tension, negative energy, and
emotions flow away from your center as you dispel them
with the breath.
You are now completely relaxed, refreshed, and alert...
Feeling better than before...
Ready to begin a new day...
The first day of the rest of your life.
Breathe in.
Slowly open your eyes.

The clever student will note that merely by breathing in and
out and visualizing the bilateral meridians that one has learned
a simple and highly effective method of remembering these
twelve meridians. This memory trick often used by Shaolin
students of Dum Mak (Death Touch) and Healing Hands. See,
we told you it was easy!

LONGEVITY EXERCISES: PART TWO

SPECIAL HEALING TECHNIQUES

The following techniques are the medicinal methods of healing the body, which ensure full range of motion, and expand the internal energy to the physical self in order to deal with the obstacles and opportunities that present themselves in daily life. They should be done as needed to deal with particular injuries, strains, or illnesses at this point in the exercise sequence, as one is arousing one's self from the Inner Journey.

Many of these movements are also found in other systems of health and longevity, most notably Hatha Yoga, which is also based on the orderly progression of Sun and Moon in their orbits as a way to explain the various functions of the human being.

Most martial arts begin by teaching how to injure the opponent, and only in the advanced stages how to revive him or tend to his wounds. Quite often this valuable information is only discovered by the student in the treatment of his own injuries received in training.

Ninjitsu, on the other hand, begins by teaching how to heal oneself, which can then be extrapolated to the healing of others, and to understand the imbalances that make others think that force or violence is any way to get what they want.

Turning The Wheel

Extend the left arm and rotate the fist thirty-six times. Follow the action of the hand with the eyes to stimulate and tone them as well. Repeat on the right side for a total of seventy-two rotations; go clockwise on the right side. This stimulates circulation in the arms and shoulders, preventing and relieving bursitis and swelling, or inflammation of the lubricating glands of the shoulder joint. The action of the left arm also stimulates and strengthens the tricuspid valve of the heart, while that of the right arm tones the mitral valve. The circular nature of this exercise represents the Wheel of Life, indicating that the Web of Heaven is a great circle, or sphere, which must eventually return to its source. So, too, is the circulation of the body. (As it is above, so below.) This exercise is a gradual reawakening of the body after the mental dream state.

Note that the action begins on the left side of the body. The heart is slightly to the left in the chest, and this exercise is designed to "start the engine" by signalling the sino-auricular nodes, which regulate the rhythm of the heartbeat, that the body is no longer in the dream state and that it is time to increase its tempo, gradually. Hydraulically, blood is squeezed from the fist and, by lifting the arm, is pulled by gravity back into the heart, which naturally must now pump harder or faster to maintain the proper flow.

Liver and Spleen Massage

Western medicine has found that man can survive with many organs atrophied or surgically removed. In fact, the degree to which a human body can withstand abuse and still function is often astounding. But no one can live without a liver. In Chinese alchemy, it represents the element Wood.

Place the right palm against the right side of the body and the left palm in the lap. With some slight pressure, trace the line of the ribcage with the heel of the hand, inhaling up to the solar plexus and exhaling down the other side, while the left hand crosses to the left side. Reverse hands, on the left side with the right hand in the lap, and breathe while massaging the spleen, just as the previous action massages the liver on the right. Repeat thirty-six times on each side, alternating sides for a total of seventy-two.

Turning the Wheel

Liver and Spleen Massage

Heart Pump

Earth Moving

Heart Pump

The heart is never toned directly. Recalling that the heart lies slightly to the left in the chest cavity, close the left fist loosely, so that the pulse will be slightly stronger, and close the fingers of the right hand around its thumb. Relax and feel for the pulses, or gently squeeze the fists. Imagine the flow of Qi in the Yin and Yang Yu Channel for the arms. Breathe in as it flows up the back of the arms and out as it flows down the inside of the arms to the palms. This stimulates the flow of blood entering the heart through the vena cava and being pumped out through the aorta. Focus your attention on the fists and synchronize your breathing with the rotation. (A previous exercise, "Turning the Wheel," also called "The Pulley," uses the less pronounced action of the right arm to strengthen the mitral valve of the heart. "Turning the pulley" with the left fist tones the tricuspid valve.) Squeezing the thumb is the palmar pump, an auxiliary to the heart pump. By placing the feet together and pressing the soles, this forms the pedal pump, back-up to the sacral pump. (The Butterfly exercise is given later.) So there are five pumps which relate to each of the five elements. The cranial pump, lest it be forgotten, is number five.

Earth Moving

The stomach is a hollow, Yang organ representing the Earth element. The pulse for this organ is found on the right wrist in acupuncture. It is moderately stimulated by the Spleen Massage. This exercise is used to tone and heal the stomach by isometric means.

Begin by placing the left hand over the organ, which is located anatomically just beneath the line of the ribcage. With the fingertips on the centerline and the thumb against the ribs, the cupped palm naturally covers the desired area. Place the right hand atop the left and exhale. Feel the warmth and relaxation from the hands penetrate the body and direct the attention to the work at hand. This single exercise insures the general health of the digestive tract. Repeat seven times—but no more than that. Overdoing the exercise can create excess gas or belching.

Stomach Healing

This exercise helps to heal the stomach and cure many ills such as flatulence (belching), overacidity, and ulcers.

Inhale as you push the right hand away from the abdomen. Concentrate on the movement. Press the palm as if pushing against a solid wall or moving a large object. Visualize the negative energy which would injure the body as being forced out through the right palm, while positive healing energy enters and churns within the organ—the imagination is the key to healing. Exhale and let the right hand drift back to cover the left. The isometric tension of this action tenses the muscles surrounding and supporting the stomach as a mild form of exercise. This simultaneously develops the ability to direct Qi, the vital Life Force, but must be done carefully to avoid injury. Repeat seven times. Earth Moving and Stomach Healing are always done together as if they were one exercise.

Deep Muscle Relaxation

Inhale deeply and completely, filling the lungs from bottom to top as you let the hands, palms downward, "float" up slightly above shoulder level. Imagine the breath being drawn deep into the Hara, the seat of breathing, and churning with the vital energy of the Life Force. Listen for the sound of the wind in your lungs, filling and expanding them with *prana*; feel the sensation of lightness in the arms flowing throughout the body, warming and healing through relaxation. Visualize the Qi rising inside the spinal column as the hands are lifted. Inhale through the nose.

In Tai Chuan, the Grand Ultimate Fist, these movements are performed while standing and are known as Establishing the Root.

Stomach Healing

Deep Muscle Relaxation

Lowering the Center

Tending the Coals

Lowering the Center

Exhale, letting the air be gently expelled between slightly parted lips, and empty the lungs from top to bottom, as if pouring water out of a glass. Imagine the diaphragm as a great bellows, slowly pushing the breath out. As the hands are lowered, visualize the energy which traveled up the spine now flowing down the front of the body. Isometrically tense each muscle group in order as the palms come down, ending with total tension in the entire body as they pass the Hara. Repeat seven times.

This exercise alternately tenses and relaxes the muscles, leading to a state of mild fatigue. Upon completion of these movements and a resumption of quiet, meditative breathing, one becomes aware of a distinct sensation of relaxation and an awareness of the total being, body and mind. The exercise relieves stress, cures constipation and diarrhea, and strengthens the spinal column.

Tending the Coals

By far the best exercise for toning the kidneys is Kindling the Fire, given previously. It is an example of a type of Yang, or positive massage, which enhances the circulation and function of the organ. This exercise is the Yin, or sedation, technique. It is used to pump blood, albeit a small amount, into the kidneys to "flush" them. In Chinese alchemy, this is symbolically represented as a secondary massage of the fire in the lower belly, hence the name. Begin by exhaling as fully as possible. Clasp the hands behind the back and interlock the fingers, drop the chin and bend slightly forward while you lift the double fist. This action squeezes the latissimus dorsi and presses blood into the lower back. Hold this position while taking six deep breaths. In Hatha Yoga, this *asana* is called Yoga Mudra.

The Small Heavenly Cycle

(Cranial Pump)   In the alchemical symbolism, the Juice of Jade has now been brought to a boil and the distilled Qi is ready

to rise to the head. Breathe in and let the energy rise up the back to the neck. Tip the head slightly back and press or touch the tip of the tongue to the roof of the mouth. Breathe out and let the energy flow down the front of the body, back to the center. Tip the head forward and press or touch the tip of the tongue to the roof of the mouth. This is the Small Heavenly Cycle of the Golden Elixir, which promotes good health and longevity; through it one learns to breathe slowly and deeply, even in times of stress, providing the user with a calm mind and a healthy body.

Opening the Lotus

(Butterfly Exercise/Pedal or Foot Pump)   Having completed the exercises up to this point, or upon finishing as much of the set as needed, it becomes necessary to stimulate circulation in the legs. Zen students often sit for hours. Americans call this the "school of aching legs meditation." If the Lotus is used, begin by lifting the left ankle off the right upper thigh, or merely lean forward and adjust the legs apart. Rub the feet and toes with the hands to promote circulation to the extremities; then rub the soles of the feet together. Draw the heels of both feet together inward as near the pelvis as possible. Steadily press down on the thighs with the elbows, intending to gradually push the knees to the floor. This action opens the pelvic girdle. Next stroke the inside of the thighs, upward from the knees, with the palms to increase the flow of blood to the hips. This exercise also improves flexibility in the knees and ankles, as well as tones the spleen, liver, kidney, and sexual glands. Repeat seven times.

Knee Relaxation

Continue to relax the legs by cupping the knees in each hand and lifting them together in front of the chest, with the soles resting on the floor. Rub the knees in a circular motion from inside the kneecap to the outside forty-nine times. Gently press

The Small Heavenly Cycle

Opening the Lotus

Knee Relaxation

Chest Warming

the knees together with the palms for a few seconds, then relax completely.

For cramps of the calf, press with the ball of the thumb on the acupuncture point known as San Ti, located in the lateral proximal fossa of each tibia, three times as you exhale. Then massage the gastroenemius muscle up and down forty-nine times with the warmed palms.

Concentrate on the knees and the soles of the feet. The science of healing the body by manipulation of the feet is known as reflexology, which employs a map of the feet much like the map of the hands given earlier.

Chest Warming

Pull the knees as close as is comfortable to the chest and encircle them with the arms. Hold the opposite elbows with each hand and "hug" the folded legs. Exhale fully and completely, dropping the head to the knees and turning the shoulders in, allowing the back to curl. This pose brings the thighs against the anterior surface of the body, and is used in arctic climes to conserve body heat. The breath can be warmed and circulated in the chamber formed by the position. The thighs warm the chest and the carbon dioxide content of the recycled air lowers both respiration and heartbeat, thus slowing the metabolism and further conserving energy. Likewise, this gentle squeezing action acts as a warming massage to the entire torso.

Lower Back Stretch

Inhale slowly and deeply, filling the lungs and raising the head at the same time to elevate the head and stretch the vertebrae of the neck. As the lungs and lower abdomen fill with air, the torso will naturally pull away from the legs to allow for the expansion. This movement lifts the ribcage upward, thus straightening the lumbar vertebrae and aligning any discrepancies in the lower back. This opens the Middle Gate, allowing the

Qi to rise upward and enter the skull by passing through the Gate of Jade, in the neck. Likewise, it acts secondarily on the kidneys. Repeat seven times.

This exercise also improves digestion and is the foundation of the Yogic Squatting Pose.

Leg Extension

Lean back from the Lotus Position and place the palms flat on the mat slightly behind the body. Lean back, setting the elbows and straightening the back. Point the toes and extend the legs directly in front. Set the heels down softly and relax the knees. Push up gently with the arms, lifting the torso easily. This aligns the vertebrae of the lower back, hips, and sacrum. The weight of the pelvis exerts a gentle traction on the spine.

Like the channels of Qi, all of the nerves, linked together synaptically, provide for the flow of nerve impulses and vital Life Force as surely as the veins and arteries circulate blood. By stimulating this network at any one point, one obviously affects all of the interrelated parts. Therefore, the ancients have said that to stimulate the feet is to tone all the organs of the body. Wiggling and manipulating the toes requires concentration and practice as well. This is the first step in learning the Nine Steps of Ninjitsu. In time, one learns to use the feet like the legendary Harry Houdini, to untie knots and pick locks, of course, such a skill is not learned in a day.

Leg Straightening

Place the hands on either side of the hips. Exhale as you bend forward, sliding the hands down the outside of the legs. Press the head to your knees. Again, this massages the abdomen. The importance of this cannot be overstated. Extend the fingers around the outsides of the feet and hold the edges for a few seconds. Inhale and sit back up slowly, sliding the hands up the insides of the thighs. This stretches the arms as well as the legs, and tones the muscles of both sets of limbs. It will make the legs straight and beautiful. Perform this exercise twelve times.

Lower Back Stretch

Leg Extension

Leg Straightening

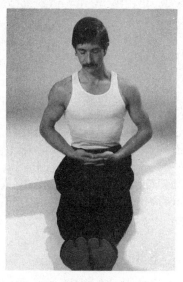

Breath Cleansing

Breath Cleansing

To remove toxins and stale air from the lungs and promote general health, perform the following movements nine times. Interlock the fingers with thumbs touching and place the cupped hands in the lap. Concentrate on the "seat of breathing," the Hara, a point two inches below the navel on the lower abdomen. Inhale fully and deeply, filling the lungs bottom to top. Imagine pure, white, healing, purifying air entering the body and being drawn into the Hara as the hands are slowly raised to chin level. Inhale through the nose.

Breathing Out

With the hands at throat level, turn them over and exhale as you push upward isometrically. Imagine a gray mist of negative energy being forced out of the body and the lungs being filled with a healing blue color like clear sky. (Do not underestimate the power of visualization in healing the body.) Holding the exhalation, once again lower the hands into the lap to repeat the cycle. Breathing in and breathing out together form the exercise known as Two Hands Uphold the Sky.

Two Hands Uphold the Sky

This exercise may be done sitting or standing. Having lifted the Qi from the Hara to the throat while inhaling, fingers interlocked and palms up, turn the hands over and push upward as you exhale. Relax, and let the arms settle back to the lap. Repeat nine times. This is one of the most basic movements of all exercise regimens. It is used to stretch and align the vertebrae from the coccyx to the skull. And like the others since Turning the Wheel, it represents a slow and gradual return to full waking consciousness.

Touch the Toes

Another of the basic movements is to bend forward. Any such action naturally provides some internal massage to the diges-

Breathing Out

Two Hands Uphold the Sky

Touch the Toes

All Fours Pose

tive system, thereby improving its function. (Proper digestion and elimination are often the goals of ancient exercises.) Place the palms on the hips and slide the hands down the outside of the legs to the feet. Grasp the outside edge of the foot and hold the pose for a moment. Release and slide the hands back to the lap with the thumbs tracing along the inside of the thigh. This stimulates the Yin and Yang Yu Channels of the leg. Bending forward, breathe out and in when sitting up. Repeat twelve times.

All Fours Pose

Man is one of the few animals who stand upright. Even the great apes drop down and run on all fours. Over one's lifetime, the natural pull of gravity on the organs tends to have an effect on them. This exercise relieves this ever present pressure. In Yoga there are many postures, such as the headstand, which invert the body. In Chinese terms this "reverses the Yin and Yang" and is beneficial to the system for short periods. The Four Corners Exercise is much more subtle and less difficult to perform, but still reverses the pull of gravity.

Bend forward and assume the Seiza Position, sitting on the heels with the legs folded beneath you. Lean forward with the hands reaching out, then rock forward and balance on the hands and knees. Inhale deeply and hold for four heartbeats. Sit back on the haunches, squeezing the chest against the thighs, thus forcing blood to the head. Exhale as you do so. In this way the lungs are empty in the folded position. Repeat no more than seven times.

Sphinx Pose

Shift the weight out over the hands and lower the chest to the floor over the elbows. Bring the fingertips together to form a small triangle, and fix your attention on that for a moment. Extend the legs out behind you and touch the large toes together as well, thus forming a complete circuit through the entire body. This exercise is similar to the Serpent Pose of Hatha

Sphinx Pose

Yoga, but is much more profound. Note that the hand position is the same one used in Kuji Kiri as "Control the (five) Elements of Nature."

Look over your right shoulder at your right heel. Inhale, letting energy travel up the leg, over the hips, the back, shoulders, down the arm, and into the middle finger. Exhale, slowly pressing the Qi back down to the heel on the right side. Look over the left shoulder and repeat on that side. Do this seven times. This promotes the flow of Qi within the body, curing many illnesses and any injuries to the legs or arms.

Pushing Up

Separate the hands and bring the palms near the shoulders with elbows bent upward. Lift the eyes and head so you can watch the horizon. Inhale fully and deeply.

Push with both hands at the same time while keeping the body rigid. Pivot on the toes and let them act as a fulcrum. This exercise tones and builds the pectorals on the chest as well as

Pushing Up

Step Up

the biceps and triceps of the arms. If done on fingertips, the forearms are also developed. In addition, it improves and strengthens the posture. Exhale as you lower yourself to the mat. Repeat twelve times.

Step Up

Swing the left leg forward and place the knee up against the chest, between the arms. Arch the head up and back, as if looking toward the sky. The right knee rests on the mat, with toes flexed. Inhale as you arch backward.

Exhale and lower the head, straightening the leg back to its position next to the right. Bring the right leg up against the chest and repeat the movement on that side. This is one round. Repeat five times.

This exercise stretches the neck and extends the hips for maximum flexibility. Likewise, it flexes the joints of the knee and ankle, thereby toning the entire leg.

Sun Contemplation

Bring first the left foot, then the right, side by side with knees bent and hands beside them. The feet form a 45-degree angle.

Keeping the hands on the floor, push up with both legs, and straightening them, lift the hips vertically. Keep the head and upper body completely relaxed and "hanging loosely" from the waist. In Taoist Yoga, this position is performed with the back to the East, in the belief that the Yang energy of the sun will be beneficial to the lower colon, and concurrently, the digestive system. Hold this position for three breaths.

Remember that drainage of venous blood from the head is accomplished by gravity, so do not hang too long lest the face become flushed and reddened. This movement also stretches the "hamstrings" on the back of each leg, allowing greater flexibility. Do not lock the knees.

Head-to-Knee

Reach behind the legs with both hands, grasping the large tendon at the lower end of the calf muscles in each palm. Pull the forehead to the knees slowly and evenly twelve times.

This exercise provides a greater extension for the hamstrings, as well as compressing the lower abdomen to act as a gentle massage for the lower muscles.

The Head-to-Knee posture has long been known in Hatha Yoga, and may be performed in the seated position with equally good results as in Touch the Toes.

Sun Contemplation

Head-to-Knee

Arching Back

Put the palms together, and "open" them so that only the thumbs and index fingers touch. Extend the thumbs so that a small triangular window is formed between the fingers.

Inhale fully and deeply as you arch backwards, lifting the window over the head and following the movement with the eyes. Hold the stretch for a few seconds, then relax and exhale slowly as you bring the hands back down in front of the solar plexus and turn the palms together.

Prayer Pose

The hands are a microcosm of the body, just as the body is a microcosm of the Universe. Each finger represents a specific element in the Five Element theory.

In Kuji Kiri meditation, the fingers are knit together in a certain mystic configuration to "connect" the meridians of acupuncture which flow in the hands. In men, the energy of these pathways is electric; in women the energy is magnetic. In

Arching Back   **Prayer Pose**

either, fingerknitting permits the Qi to be directed for medicinal or psychological purposes. This pose joins each with its corresponding partner to insure a proper flow in the body.

The Sun Salute

In Hatha Yoga (of India) all adepts are required to know the Sun Salute. The Hindu name for this set of movements is Soorya Namaskar, and it is practiced for general health and well-being. It is composed, essentially, of the last seven exercises, performed in the following sequence: 1) Palms Together; 2) Arch Back; 3) Head-to-Knee; 4) Step Back (Up); 5) Push-Up; 6) The Sphinx Pose; 7) Push-Up again; 8) Step Up (right foot); 9) Head-to-Knee; 10) Arch Back; 11) Return to Prayer Pose. This similarity of applied kinesthesiology and philosophy points to a commonality of origin in the two systems. Some believe these were known to the most ancient civilizations and spread with the growth of mankind, being lost to some and modified by others. Still they have remained, and have been documented existing as long ago as 6000 B.C.

Observe how the system of exercises in this book has progressed logically from the Dream State, lying down or sleeping postures; to sitting, the exercise of stillness; to various movements and regulation of breathing in Qi Gong; to stretching and standing, in the Sun Salute.

THE DA MO SERIES

The Da Mo Series of exercises has also been called the Muscle Change Classic. The series is reported to have been a set of movements taught to the Shaolin Monks when Bodhiharma came across the mountains from India to China and found the Shaolin to be spiritually sound but physically weak. Others attribute them to a particular general of the ancient Chinese army, who toughened his men with the isometric motions and dynamic tension. Naturally, the ability to stand firmly is essential to both the warrior and the mystic. Therefore, at the conclusion of the Da Mo Set of Twelve, the technique of Rooting is taught. This is also the first exercise in Tai Chi Chuan, one of the internal styles of martial art, which employs visualization and energy channeling to enhance the power and balance of the student's technique.

The Da Mo exercises are employed to develop the circulation of internal energy in the physical body for strength of mind and body. One begins them where one ended the Sun Salute—in the Prayer Pose.

It is interesting to note that the position of standing in the Prayer Pose is symbolized by the first Kuji Kiri mudra, i.e., the middle fingers extended and all the others folded. Since the middle fingers represent the Fire element, it follows that making this mudra, which symbolizes the Prayer Pose, means one has taken the first of Nine Steps in the study of Ninjitsu. Thus, the "invocation" of strength of mind and body, which is associated with the first mudra (extended middle fingers), is culminated by reaching this first step in the development of one's Self. In an infant it is represented by standing up instead

127

of crawling around on the floor like an animal. (The Fire element is also symbolized as sexual energy from the prostate gland, which we are elevating, along with our spiritual consciousness, from base desires to loftier goals than mere procreation—indeed, onward to creation of a harmonious world by setting a good example.)

Having purified the mind and body with these exercises, one is ready for step two, Direction of Energy. This is symbolized by the second mudra, middle fingers around the index, which is an entire set of standing in place exercises. The Da Mo Series is the first.

This, then, is not only how the exercises come full circle, returning to the beginning, but also how each psychological step "suggested" on the internal level during meditation becomes, and relates to, an entire body building program.

It is said that, with sufficient practice, the masters no longer needed even these movements to maintain themselves, since they had "programmed their internal computers" to the point where the mere touching of their fingers in forming the first Kuji Kiri mudra would immediately begin the circulation developed by these techniques. This is the basis for legends that, in times of stress or danger, the Ninja would calm themselves by making the Kuji In-signs, to draw on their "magical" power.

The real masters, however, were those who had long since given up adventuring into battle and thus passed beyond the need for even the mudras. It was enough for them to merely think of the "energy wheel" or chakra or pump (5) in question to set it spinning and derive its benefit.

There are two kinds of strength: the outer, which is apparent and fades with age; and the inner, which is unseen and is eternal. Once we have acquired self-knowledge and an understanding of the way of Nature, it is clearly evident that no one can control the actions of another. In fact, if we can control our own wants and needs, let alone our fears and desires, we shall have accomplished a great deal. When that is possible, we shall glow with the vitality and energy of inner peace, and no longer seek to control others, or even to interfere in their lives by giving advice.

Seeking only to improve ourselves, we shall be seen as good examples to follow; and divesting ourselves of petty ambition to pursue this great goal, we shall be known as followers of peace, and therefore nonthreatening, unlikely to feel the need for power over others. In this way, power can be achieved because others, motivated by self-interest, will want to know how to do the things we have learned and are about to learn herein. And when they ask, we must tell them freely, and share all that we have, so that they too can find the Way.

Contained within these pages are the most profound and ancient exercises ever recorded. Do not begin them lightly, or without proper respect, for they are powerful in the extreme, and will most certainly change your life for the better. Once begun, 'tis done. There can be no going back to the past, nor leaping forward to the future—only the reality of now.

These movements will balance the flow of energy in the body, thereby healing old wounds and filling the self with vitality. That is their first benefit. It is often said, "What good are all the treasures of the Earth, if one does not have health?" This will give you Health.

But not immediately, of course. The effects of all yogic postures, like those of meditation, are cumulative. One starts and before long notices that it has been weeks since the first day. Then suddenly some ache or pain that was obvious at the outset seems much improved or has vanished altogether. Surely the rewards of daily exercise for the maintenance and well-being of the body are worth a few minutes of our time. Surely you did not expect to read chapter one and have instant mind control over the masses. Whatever effort would have been put into that goal can be much better spent on the improvement of one's Self, a far nobler mission, to be certain.

The second benefit of these techniques is the gradual ability to direct, or conversely act in accordance with, the flow of energy within the physical body. With this power one may transcend the lower levels of consciousness, which impede progress toward the realization of one's true nature and place in the Universe.

NEI KUNG: INTERNAL STRENGTH

Prolonged practice of the internal exercises shown herein enables the practitioner to gain some degree of control over his or her physical being. When this is accomplished, the *genin*, or lower Self, is quieted and calmed, which permits liberation of the higher levels of being. Note, that in Ninjitsu, "genin" is also the term for the field agent, and indicates to the higher ranks (*chunin* and *jonin*) that the person so designated is not above the third level of comprehension, and so is concerned with survival and conquest rather than peace and harmony.

Control of the body leads to control of the mind. When one knows how to do anything, the impossible becomes commonplace. To do, to demonstrate it for the edification of others, is an expression of Ego. There is no need to "prove" one's power to anyone other than oneself. Those who have it, know it; those who do not can never recognize it.

There is no "proof" of anything, only lessons and tests. And one must choose to be present for them.

Control of the Body

By concentrating on one's breathing, the mind becomes aware of internal sounds. In time this develops into the ability to withdraw the consciousness from the physical being to the inner sanctum and fortress of the mind. In such a state of meditative balance, the body is sustained and protected by the energized electromagnetic aura which Western science has only recently acknowledged.

1. Having completed the Sun Salute, (the last of the Longevity Exercises described in the last section), lower the palms from the Prayer Pose and hold them palms down at the sides. Sink the Qi to the Hara and exhale completely. Inhale, slowly and deeply, drawing the air deep into the belly; tighten the seat muscles and lift the

fingers upward. Let the energy rise up the spine and feel it in the forearms. Hold for three heartbeats, then relax and let the fingertips relax slightly. Repeat no less than three nor more than nine times.

2. Close the fingers into a loose fist, but with the thumbs extended. Hold them at the level of the Hara. Relax as before, then inhale with dynamic tension in the Hara—meaning with seat muscles squeezed together to activate the sacral pump—and raise the energy up the insides of the arms and up the front of the body. Hold as before, and relax. Likewise, repeat three to nine times. (Figure 39)

3. Fold the fingers around the thumbs to prevent the Qi from leaking out, and to circulate the energy in the channels of the arms. Move the fists back beside the hips and, breathing as before, squeeze the fists as if pressing downward. The energy rises up the front and back channels, circulates in the head on the inhalation, and lowers through the Jen and Tu Mo back to the Hui Yin point on the perineum, just as in the Small Heavenly Cycle of the seated meditation. (Figure 40)

   Some schools advocate that the feet be alternately held slightly apart, then together in each of the postures, but the oldest known records of these exercises teach that one should keep the feet slightly apart throughout. Therefore, one may separate the feet at the beginning of the Da Mo Series, or hold them as in the Attention, or Pillar Pose, or take turns, as desired. The important thing is to tense the entire body when pressing in the indicated direction to open the channels and pull the Qi through the body. The Tai Chi Chuan Players have a saying: "Channeling Qi is like trying to push a string; it cannot be done. But an ant can pull a thread through the hollow of a pearl with ease. This is the method."

4. Hold the fists vertically at shoulder level and breathe as before, tensing and relaxing in turn, while pressing the forearms out to the sides as if pushing them against the sides of a doorway. (Figure 41)

FIGURE 39

FIGURE 40

FIGURE 41

FIGURE 42

5. Raise the arms in a wide circular movement outward until they are parallel and overhead. Breathing as before, pull downward on the tension part of the cycle. This circulates the Qi throughout the entire body. Repeat three to nine times. (Figure 42)

6. Lower the fists until they are near the ears and form a triangle, with the apex being at the top of the head and the bent elbows forming the sides. Breathing as described, pull the elbows backward three to nine times with dynamic tension. This strengthens the elbows, wrists, and forearms. The idea is not so much to strain or marshal intense effort when performing these exercises. Rather, a relaxed attitude is more conducive to proper circulation. Only slight tension should be used to initiate the Qi movement. Then the mind will guide the breath through the channel. The Qi, being electromagnetic in nature, follows the direction of the mind and breath and travels along the sympathetic and parasympathetic nervous systems. (Figure 43)

7. Extend the fists vertically out to the sides, without locking the elbows, and pull the fist backward while breathing in the prescribed manner three to nine times. Then raise up alternately on the left and right toes twelve times. This stimulates and promotes internal harmony among the vital organs. Just as there are channels in the arms, the legs contain the Yin (inside) and Yang (outside) Chiao Mo, or Leg Channels. These flow up the inside of the leg on the inhalation and down the outside to the edge of the foot on the exhalation. (Figure 44)

8. Bring the arms in laterally with the fists held vertically at shoulder level and the arms parallel. Using the same breathing technique, press the fists forward while lifting the heels slightly. Relax and lower the heels to the surface. This movement trains the arms to draw Qi from the Hara. In the more advanced levels of these exercises, the palms are used to direct the Qi around the body and beyond. In this way it may be transmitted from the

center of the palm when a strike is made. This is why the old masters would spar with each other with their fists closed (since the palm is the primary weapon of the Ninja). That way they could not transmit the killing power of their Qi to a strike. (Figure 45)

9. Bend the elbows and bring the fists forward toward the face. Pull the elbows back while turning the fists over and out. Repeat three to nine times. This toughens the forearms and opens both the lung channels and those that flow on the inside of the arms. Remember to perform these exercises slowly and with slight dynamic tension in the Hara area. If practiced over a long period of time, the cumulative effect will encourage the flow of Qi along the most efficient path. (Figure 46)

10. Carry the arms out from the sides of the head with elbows bent, as if lifting a heavy weight overhead in the military press technique. Face the palms to the front while maintaining the fists around thumb as in the previous techniques. Hold the forearms vertically, and pull the bent arms back while breathing as before. Repeat three to nine times per session. (Figure 47)

11. With feet together, return the arms to the position in front of the Hara shown in figure 39, and extend the thumbs as in that movement. Clench the fists slightly and lift the thumbs while raising the fists to navel level. You should feel the Qi creeping up the insides of the arms. This exercise permits the Qi to rise and fall within the body.

12. Let the fingers hang loosely for a moment, then, while raising up on the toes, lift the hands palm uppermost with fingers out to shoulder level. Hold with slight dynamic tension, then relax and let the heels come to earth and the arms lower to the thighs. Repeat twelve times. This exercise relaxes the sinews and acts to restore balance to the flow of Qi within the body after the set of twelve Da Mo movements. (Figure 48)

FIGURE 43

FIGURE 44

FIGURE 45

FIGURE 46

FIGURE 47   **FIGURE 48**

Establishing the Root

Having moved from a state of quiet, seated contemplation, and slowly advanced to a balanced, standing position, you can use this movement to mark the transition from the Dream-Time to full waking consciousness, the state of Reality. It has been said that the test of reality is touch. The eyes may be deceived, the ears confused, the mind clouded, but touch is certain.

It has been said that there is a web of Heaven, and an ebb and flow to its existence. And now you will touch that web, feel its pulse, and become part of it.

Qi is the universal Life Force. It flows through us, around us, and within us, always. To become aware of it, one must relax, and wait.

From the previous position, step with the left foot so that the feet are slightly more than shoulder width apart. (This too, follows the pattern of Yin and Yang. A man should always step off with his left foot first, a woman step back with her right foot as if dancing.)

Point the toes straight ahead, with the knees slightly bent and the hips slid backward as if riding a horse. (This is the foundation of the Horse Riding Stance found in every martial art known to man. It is used to develop superior strength in the thigh, hip, and calves by training the legs to stand for long hours in a single isometrically tensed position. But not one in a thousand martial artists knows its origin or its real function: channeling the Life Force to develop Iron Body, harness the powers of Dim Mak [death touch] and the Healing Touch, enhance fighting ability, or enable the Ninja to disappear or fly without wings.)

The back is straight, the shoulders square, and the eyes are fixed leisurely on a spot slightly forward on the ground. Let the arms hang loosely in front of the hips, with hands relaxed.

With palms down, inhale slowly and deeply, filling the lungs from bottom (Hara) to top. Let the hands float upward to shoulder level to simulate the breath entering the body, as if the wrists were suspended by strings, and follow the movement with your eyes. Raise the right big toe.

Imagine the Qi rising from the Great Earth Mother, up the inside of the right leg (Yin Yu), to the Tan T'ien (Hara) and circulating there as you complete the inhalation.

Turn the head slowly to the left and let the hands, still palms downward, sink back to waist level. Imagine the Qi, having been circulated in the center of balance and gravity, descend down the outside of the right leg to the arch of the foot. Grip the ground with your toes and lock the seat muscles as you complete the exhalation. Lower the right big toe.

Relax. Let the head return to face front and the eyes return to their relaxed gaze.

Repeat the movement on the left side. Inhaling, bring the Qi up the inside of the left leg to the center, watching the hands as they float upward, lifting the left big toe. Then, exhaling, look to the right as the hands sink to waist level and the energy flows down the outside of the left leg and the toes grip the Earth like the root of a tree.

Relax. Let the head return to face front, and perform the movement a third time.

As the hands float up, as if suspended by strings at the wrist, bring the Qi up the inside channels of both legs, to meet the energy drawn into the Hara by the inhalation. The head does not turn on this part of the exercise, nor are the toes raised, but the eyes do follow the action of the hands. In the first two steps, turning the head prevents any possibility of secretly looking at the leg when directing the Qi up and down. One must use the mind to accomplish this purpose, in harmony with the body, lifting the big toes help this.

Exhale, and let the Qi flow down the outside of both legs to the edge of both feet, gripping the ground with your toes. Tighten the seat muscles and maintain dynamic tension in the Hara. This is the real secret to overcoming the muscle cramps and aches that invariably result in beginning the practice. After a while, the body adapts and one can stand for hours. By these means, the legs are made healthy and strong.

Concentrate on the One-Point, the lower Tan T'ien. All movement must come from this site. In Tai Chi Chuan, the Grand Ultimate Fist, it is said, "the waist is the banner, it goes into battle first." This lends some credence to the theory that all martial arts are based on Tai Chi Chuan, since, even in such Japanese systems as Shotokan Karate, all power is derived from the hips, and students are taught to move these largest muscles in the body as the initial stage of almost every technique. This conforms to good body mechanics, since they are the center of gravity for the body, and explains the samurai tradition and motto: "when you are afraid, tighten your belly and charge!"

Practice deep breathing, and imagine the soles of your feet "rooted" to the Earth, drawing energy and life from the source of Yin.

Tree Hugging Exercise

Now that the root has been established, it is time to feel the pulse of the Universe. This is accomplished by means of the Tree Hugging Exercise.

At the completion of the previous exercise, relax. Breathe in, and let the Qi rise from the Earth, up the inside of the legs to the One-Point, back to the coccyx at the base of the spine, up the back to the Wind Gate (between the shoulder blades), where it divides and passes down the outside of the arms to the hands, back up the inside of the arms to the center of the back, up the back of the neck, around the ears, and over the top of the head to the Ming Tang, or Third Eye.

At the same time, let the hands float upward to solar plexus level, with the palms facing inward and the arms relaxed and rounded. Fix the gaze slightly above and beyond the fingertips.

Without further movement, relax and breathe out, letting the Qi flow down the front of the face, neck, chest, and belly, to the One-Point, where it divides and travels down the outside of both legs, back to the edge of the feet.

Feel the pulse beating in your palms.

Continue this cycle of inhalation up the inside of the legs and back, down and up the arms, up around the ears, and over the head, then down the front of the body and the outside of the legs, as you exhale for as long as comfortable. Note that this is the exact position one would assume if one were to wrap his arms around a large tree and press oneself against it. Hence the name.

No great emphasis should be placed on exactly how far apart the legs are, or how rounded the arms, or lowered the shoulders, as these things will soon adjust themselves to fit the student perfectly, and then the position will be correct.

In ancient times this method was used by martial artists to teach their students the need for patience and to confirm the flow of the Universe, since inevitably after some hours of practice they would return to the teacher with the revelation that they had "felt the heartbeat of the tree in their hands, and become one with the Universe."

Directing, or flowing with, the Qi in this manner is called the Grand Circulation of Energy or Large Heavenly Cycle, it is distinguished from the previous Small Heavenly Cycle, used to unite the Jen Mo and Tu Mo in preparation for the Eight Psychic Channels Exercise, which leads to this one.

Thus the Qi is collected, cultivated, and circulated into a single point—which is everywhere at once.

BODY OF IRON

Ninja have been called the ultimate warriors. But it is not we who have said this. The basis for the legendary exploits of the feudal Ninja clans of Japan do not even begin to touch the powers and abilities of the true mystic-warrior. Yet they provide some insight into the philosophical and historical foundations upon which the Silent Way is based.

It is called the Silent Way because it is not spoken of. Not because it is a secret, but because the answer is different for each person, though the techniques may be the same.

Followers of Ninjitsu are taught many skills, and, by learning them, they find the Way for themselves. One example of this, and one sorely neglected in most martial arts training, is meditation.

Meditation is part of what is meant by "one must be strong, one must know, one must dare, and one must be silent," a common injunction given to Ninjitsu students. Many beginning students believe that being strong is merely a physical phenomenon. But remember, there are two kinds of strength, the external, which is obvious and fades with age, and the internal strength of will, which takes much longer to cultivate, but lasts a lifetime.

How is it a Ninja could withstand kicks and punches that would fell an ordinary man? How were they able to fight on and prevail, despite impossible odds? The same way the Shaolin monks were able to endure torture at the hands of ruthless emperors when captured. The same way they have trained themselves to live in and even enjoy the most inhospitable of snowy mountain retreats—by doing these very exercises,

140

the Da Mo Series, or by whatever name they may be known in whatever system or style is teaching them.

This art and these techniques are far older than their Japanese counterparts. They are often taught in Kung Fu schools as Iron Shirt or Iron Vest breathing exercises, but they are still the same as the Pranayama techniques of Hindu Yoga.

No one "owns" these methods, although they have been concealed by a number of agencies for a variety or reasons.

Here, then, in this chapter, are the Iron Body exercises, which, as promised by Ko Hung, will make you invulnerable to serpent's fang and tiger's claw. They are not taught in other "Ninjitsu" schools because these schools do not know them—although they will doubtless claim some form of proprietorship upon publication of this material.

THE IRON BODY EXERCISE

By means of this technique, the Ninja is able to achieve a state of suspended animation which makes the body impervious to injury and slows the effect of disease or poison. While in this cataleptic mode, the individual is still aware of his surroundings; thus, any mistreatment will be experienced, but without harm being done. The duration of this ability is dependent upon the skill of the user. (Figure 49)

Stand in the Classic Pillar Stance, heels together, feet at a 45-degree angle, arms at sides, fingers loosely curled, eyes closed. Inhale deeply, then exhale half the volume of air. Lower the chin, hold the breath. Imagine the Yin energy rising from the heels, up the legs to chest, up the arms to the head. Visualize the circulation of Qi within the body. (Figure 50)

Fold the arms across the chest in the manner of the Egyptian Mummy Pose. The body is now entirely rigid, so rigid in fact that it may be suspended by the head and feet between two points for extended periods, and heavy weights may even be placed on the chest without injury. (Figure 51)

This is the foundation of all Iron Body techniques and exercises. It is helpful to envision an iron bar or rod within the

 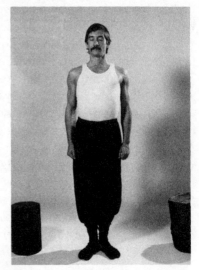

FIGURE 49   **FIGURE 50**

spine during the early stages of practice. *Do not try this alone* or without at least three months practice on the floor or mat.

Depending on the degree of mastery of the student, this state may be maintained for as long as concentration permits. This allows the user to withstand extremes of heat and cold unbearable for the untrained, to breathe underwater, be buried alive, or walk through flames unharmed. Fakirs who walk on hot coals or sit on beds of nails are demonstrating this power.

With more experience, the disciple may develop superior balance, which will allow him to adjust the weight of his body by muscular tension. This makes it possible to walk tightwires, climb walls, move silently, and fall without injury. The art of *ukemi* (Judo break-falling) is based on this, as well as the magical technique of expanding or reducing the size of the body. The best example of this was the famous Houdini, who "puffed up" his chest when being bound with ropes; then relaxed and had sufficient slack to wriggle free of the bonds. Conversely, the Hindu who folds himself into a trunk or jar which appears too small to contain him illustrates reduction.

FIGURE 51

With this mental control, any part of the body can withstand injury without harm and may be equally useful as a weapon. In ancient texts these are referred to as the Iron Body styles and require *kime* (focus) and *genshin* (balance).

Naturally, all this requires an expenditure of energy. In China, the ability to work steadily on a task to its completion without regard for food or water is highly valued. Meditation enables one to calm these callings temporarily, but an equal amount of time must be spent replenishing the source. This power makes it possible to suspend all outward appearance of life and not awaken until the user desires, to heal one's own wounds, and forestall the effects of poison.

Lazy Iron Body

As with all true magic, those who can, do, and don't speak about it. Those who can't, fake it. There have always been those who sought to emulate the ways of the masters, without going through the process required to attain a mystic power.

For example, when the White Lotus Sect of China decided around 1890 that there were too many foreign devils in the country and staged an uprising known as the Boxer Rebellion, they did not have time to train all their followers in the esoteric methods of internal energy, nor were they all that eager to share the philosophical underpinnings of their clique. So they settled on the next best method: trickery.

It was not uncommon, in those days, for martial artists to perform publicly, demonstrating their skills for the contributions of an admiring crowd. Thus, it was not unheard of for a mystery school to present a demonstration by its senior students. The White Lotus Sect would present these shows with men eating burning incense, walking on hot coals, being hit with timbers, and chopped with swords without suffering any injury. The big finale was when the high priest stopped a bullet with his "iron body." (The weaponry of the day was still pretty primitive, but a musket ball could still be deadly.)

So, wearing his "magic shirt amulet," the priest would have one of the senior students, whom he could trust, shoot him in the chest. When he was not killed, he ripped away his "magic" vest, concealing the sheet of iron he had previously sewn in to stop the bullet, and showed there was no mark. The believers were stunned! Assured that they, too, could possess this magic power for a small donation, and would then be invulnerable enough to drive foreign devils out of the homeland, did they join? You bet they did! And hundreds of them in human waves ran screaming to their deaths against withering gunfire, until the devils were overcome and driven from China; every one was falsely secure in the knowledge that his "magic shirt amulet" would protect him, and that if his fellows died despite the magic, it was because they did not believe strongly enough.

It should be noted that the Shaolin monks also experimented with this form of Iron Shirt Kung Fu. So certain were they of their ability to control breath and tissue that they sacrificed scores of young monks willing to see if their "iron body" could stop a bullet.

They would stand in line, muskets leveled at their chests, performing the exercises that protected them from bruises and pain, and recite the mantra, "Kung Fu is stronger than bullets!" in a loud voice. Then they would be shot, usually in the chest. The abbot or high priest would then walk quickly down the line, slapping magic paper amulets upon the wounds, and stop at the far end to observe the reaction of the students. Of course the result was invariably the same: the students could stand by will alone, and by virtue of the stance they had assumed, sometimes for several minutes. But, eventually, they all fell over and died.

The monks had not yet grasped the fact that bullets flew at a much greater velocity than did the arrows of the day, many of which were not fatal because the Iron Body did indeed prevent them from penetrating enough to affect internal organs.

Fortunately, the Shaolin were wise enough to realize that bullets could not be stopped by skin, and so adopted other martial arts techniques, such as the Arrow Catching Set, in which the student is trained to slip out of the way and catch an arrow as it passes. When it came to bullets, of course, the operative method was to dodge them, rather than try to catch them. In Ninjitsu of modern times this is called the Bullet Dodging Kata, but it is taught in very few schools.

Another example of the Lazy Iron Body was the Japanese practice of "tying off" a uniform. This was ostensibly to tighten up the uniform so that it would not snag on anything when the warrior snuck up on the enemy castle. In reality, however, it is a method of prepositioning tourniquets so that, if one were wounded in an extremity, one need only twist the blousing ties tighter to cut off the flow of blood (remember Sasuke's tourniquet in the introduction). Even a slightly greater pressure can be used to restrict blood flow enough to make the arms and legs partially numb. That way, any kicks or punches the enemy might land will be less effective. For the sake of showmanship, it also makes the muscles "pump up" and the veins stand out, because the blood is forced to the torso to protect the internal organs, just as when doing the Iron Body Exercise properly.

The Moro tribe used this same technique when battling American soldiers in the Philippines. They would "tie them selves off," putting a tourniquet at each major joint and cluster of blood vessels, drink themselves full of "magic elixir," which had a powerful amphetamine effect, charge into a bivouac armed only with a machete and kill a couple of dozen soldiers before being brought down by rifle fire. But even then, high-

powered rifles are fired at such high velocity that at close range
the bullets often went all the way through the Moro, so that
their wounds would virtually self-seal and the tribesman
would keep fighting. The alarming frequency and effectiveness
of this type of attack was so great that the U.S. Army commis-
sioned the construction of an entirely new firearm, the .45
caliber semi-automatic pistol, which fired almost an ounce of
lead in each shot and was of low enough velocity to have
knockdown power. Once introduced to the theater of opera-
tions, these handguns soon put an end to the Moro uprising.

Still, doesn't it sound a lot like the White Lotus Sect?
Psychological indoctrination turned true believers into berserk
warriors who would throw themselves upon the enemy without regard for pain or death. So if there is any danger in
practicing Iron Body exercises (and some claim there is so they
can drive up the tuition), it is this: Those who know how to do
it will use it to trick and enslave the masses, who have less
patience. This includes the Japanese Ninja, who were known to
sew iron bars into the sleeves of their *shinobi shokozu* (uniforms)
so they could block sword cuts with a forearm.

Some schools, like Shotokan Karate, practice hand toughen-
ing exercises so the student can strike without fear. In Thai
kickboxing, they sever nerves in the leg so that one can kick
trees with full power without pain. Some Kung Fu academies
fashion an "iron broom" by taking a bundle of straightened coat
hangers and using that to flail themselves. One of the Qi Gong
tests for the Iron Shirt is to dive off an eight-foot wall and land
on your chest without getting killed.

But none of these extreme measures are necessary; all
represent the "hard" style of Iron Body. Lost and distorted are
the ancient methods of internal alchemy, which provide the
true power of good health and longevity.

So, who wants to live forever?

Here we are, born to be kings. We, the human beings, are
    the princes of the Universe. We have the blood of kings
    inside us.

We have no rivals. No one can be our equal.
We forge our lives in the fire of our will.
We have always been among you, living many lives in
many ages.
Our names are legion.
We are the chosen, the few. We are Immortal.
My name is Kim, friend to all the world.
I am the Ninja, himself, who thinks, loves, fights, and
performs the glittering magical work of the mystic
laughing light.
And that is a fact.
Looked for cannot be seen...
Listened for cannot be heard...
Felt for cannot be touched...
I come from the noplace and I go to the nowhere.
I have no magic power.
Anyone can do the things I do.
If they but know how.
It all begins with breathing.

AFTERWORD

When it was first decided to set these principles down on paper, it was decided to keep them as simple as possible, doing away with more and more, until only the key page remained, and then to reduce that to a single phrase which would encompass it all, and finally to one word that would express the entire essence.

So it was only logical that eventually even this would be put away, and a solo white sheet of paper might be all that remained. Because that is the real key—imagination. But that would hardly point the way to the Halls of Learning or the Threshold of Knowledge, so herein lies a humble effort to light that lamp and shine it upon the Path.

These things have been put down before, but they are usually clouded in mysticism. As you have seen, the reasons many of these things are expressed symbolically is because the real secret to most of them is squeezing your seat muscle together—a secret which, when revealed, "makes a grown man blush and a woman giggle." The symbolism once also served to conceal knowledge from the many (the population of peasants at large) and save it for the few (those who think they are leaders). But I have explained it for you, as clearly and simply as it is within my humble powers at this point in time. Much of the information in this book may seem vague, or couched in its own archaic language. It is, after all, only the ramblings of one who has passed this way before. But, like Machiavelli's *The Prince*, it is presented as a gift, in the hope that some good may be gleaned from it and that the lessons thus far learned by the author may be passed on to others for their consideration.

Ashida Kim
First Day, Eighth Month
Fifth Year of the Ox

148